Design Patterns in Java
Interview Questions and Answers

X.Y. Wang

Contents

4 Advanced   **131**

Chapter 1

Introduction

Design patterns are an essential aspect of software development, as they provide reusable solutions to recurring problems that developers face during the process of building applications. Having a deep understanding of design patterns not only improves the quality of the software but also the overall efficiency of the development process. In this book, "Design Patterns in Java: Interview Questions and Answers," we will cover the most important design patterns in Java, focusing on their usage, benefits, and potential challenges. Our goal is to provide a comprehensive and practical guide that not only helps you prepare for interviews but also enhances your understanding of design patterns, ultimately making you a more proficient Java developer.

The book is organized into five sections, starting with basic concepts and progressively moving towards more advanced topics. In the second chapter, we will introduce fundamental design patterns, such as Singleton, Factory Method, and Observer,

among others. This section aims to provide a solid foundation
for understanding design patterns and their roles in software
development.

In the third chapter, we will delve deeper into design patterns
and their interactions with other programming principles, such
as the Open/Closed Principle and the Dependency Inversion
Principle. We will also discuss how design patterns can be combined to create more robust and flexible systems.

The fourth chapter focuses on advanced topics, addressing the
challenges of implementing design patterns in complex and distributed systems. We will explore aspects like thread safety,
race conditions, and performance implications, providing in-
sights on how to tackle these issues effectively.

In the fifth chapter, we will discuss expert-level topics, combining design patterns with architectural concepts such as CQRS
and reactive programming. We will also analyze the trade-
offs between different patterns, providing guidance on when to
choose one pattern over another.

Finally, in the sixth chapter, we will explore design patterns
in the context of large-scale systems and microservices architectures. We will discuss the impact of design patterns on the
overall architecture, addressing factors like modularity, maintainability, and scalability.

Throughout the book, we provide real-world examples and practical advice, enabling you to apply the concepts to your projects
effectively. By the end of this book, you will have a thor-
ough understanding of design patterns in Java and will be well-
equipped to tackle software design challenges with confidence.
So, let's begin our journey towards mastering design patterns

in Java.

Chapter 2

Basic

2.1 What is a software design pattern? Can you provide a brief definition?

A software design pattern is a general, reusable solution to a commonly occurring problem in software design. It is a proven way to solve specific design problems in software engineering that has been established and documented by a community of professional developers. Design patterns are language-independent and serve as a blueprint for constructing flexible, yet robust and maintainable software systems.

At a high level, a pattern is a template or a guide on how to solve a particular software problem. It can be considered as a set of rules and guidelines that can be used to solve similar problems in different contexts. A design pattern usually consists of four main components:

- A problem description that describes the context or issue that the pattern is meant to solve.

- A solution that describes a general approach to solve the problem.

- The specific elements and their relationships that make up the solution.

- The consequences of using the pattern, including its benefits, trade-offs, and limitations.

Overall, the purpose of a pattern is to capture the knowledge and experience of software development experts and provide it to the community in a structured way, allowing developers to apply the same solutions to similar problems.

2.2   Why are design patterns important in software development?

Design patterns are important in software development as they provide a proven solution to a common design problem. They are essentially templates for solving various software design problems that have been identified by experienced developers over time. Following a design pattern helps to ensure that a software solution is efficient, reliable, and maintainable.

Below are some reasons why design patterns are important in software development:

1. Increases code reusability: Design patterns provide reusable solutions to common software design problems. Implementing a pattern ensures that the code is not only reusable within the current project but across other applications.

2. Improves maintainability: Design patterns provide a clear and well-defined structure for software development. As a result, the code is easy to maintain as modifications and updates can be easily done without making significant changes to other parts of the code.

3. Enhances scalability: Design patterns provide scalable solutions to software design problems. As the project grows, the pattern can be adapted to handle the increased complexity of the project.

4. Facilitates communication among developers: Design patterns provide a common vocabulary among developers. Teams can quickly understand the code structure, making it easier to communicate and collaborate on projects.

5. Reduces development time and cost: Design patterns provide tested and proven solutions to common software design problems. By using design patterns, developers can quickly solve problems instead of wasting time and resources trying to come up with a new solution.

Here's an example of the Singleton design pattern in Java. The Singleton pattern is used to ensure that only one instance of a class exists.

```java
public class Singleton {
    // static variable to hold the single instance of Singleton class
    private static Singleton instance = null;

    // private constructor to prevent the creation of additional
        instances of the Singleton class
    private Singleton() {
        // initialization code goes here
    }

    // public static method to get the single instance of the
        Singleton class
    public static Singleton getInstance() {
        if (instance == null) {
```

```
        instance = new Singleton();
    }
    return instance;
}

// other methods and variables below
}
```

In the code above, the Singleton class has a private constructor to prevent the creation of additional instances. The getInstance() method is used to get the single instance of the Singleton class. If the instance is null, a new instance is created, otherwise, the existing instance is returned.

By using the Singleton pattern, developers can ensure that only one instance of the class is created, which can improve performance, reduce memory usage, and prevent unexpected behavior.

2.3   Can you list the three main categories of design patterns and provide a brief explanation of each?

The three main categories of design patterns are:

1. Creational patterns: These patterns deal with the process of object creation. They aim to establish the best way to create objects to suit specific requirements. Creational patterns include:

- Singleton Pattern
- Factory Pattern
- Abstract Factory Pattern

- Builder Pattern

- Prototype Pattern

2. Structural patterns: These patterns focus on object composition, i.e., how classes and objects are designed to form larger
structures. Structural patterns include:

- Adapter Pattern

- Bridge Pattern

- Composite Pattern

- Decorator Pattern

- Facade Pattern

- Flyweight Pattern

- Proxy Pattern

3. Behavioral patterns: These patterns are associated with
how objects communicate and collaborate with each other at
runtime. Behavioral patterns include:

- Chain of Responsibility Pattern

- Command Pattern

- Interpreter Pattern

- Iterator Pattern

- Mediator Pattern

- Memento Pattern

- Observer Pattern

- State Pattern

- Strategy Pattern

- Template Method Pattern

- Visitor Pattern

I will provide a brief explanation of each of the types of design patterns:

1. Creational Patterns

These patterns are concerned with the process of object creation. They deal with the best way to create objects to suit specific requirements. The creational pattern is essential when creating objects that are complex and require a lot of setup. It is used to hide the details of object creation from the client, so the client doesn't have to worry about these details. The five types of creational design patterns are as follows:

- **Singleton Pattern**

The Singleton pattern ensures that a class has only one instance, and provides a global point of access to that instance. This pattern involves a single class, which is responsible for creating its own object, and providing access to the instance to the entire system.

- **Factory Pattern**

The Factory pattern is a creational pattern that provides an interface for creating objects in a superclass, but allows subclasses to alter the type of objects that will be created. This pattern allows a class to decide which class to instantiate at runtime.

- **Abstract Factory Pattern**

The Abstract Factory pattern is a creational pattern that provides an interface for creating related objects without specifying their concrete classes. This pattern involves a hierarchy of factories, where each factory returns a different set of related objects.

- **Builder Pattern**

The Builder pattern is a creational pattern that separates the construction of a complex object from its representation. This pattern allows you to create different representations of an object using the same construction process.

- **Prototype Pattern**

The Prototype pattern is a creational pattern that allows you to create new forms of an object by cloning from an existing instance of that object. This pattern uses an existing object as a prototype and creates a new object by copying the existing object.

2. Structural Patterns

Structural patterns deal with object composition. They aim to make it easier to combine objects into larger structures. The structural pattern describes how classes and objects are designed to form larger structures. It provides the building blocks for an application, allowing different parts of the application to work together. The seven types of structural design patterns are as follows:

- **Adapter Pattern**

The Adapter pattern converts one interface into another that the client expects. This pattern is useful when you want to make an existing class work with another class, but its interface does not match.

- **Bridge Pattern**

The Bridge pattern decouples an abstraction from its implementation. This pattern involves an abstraction that depends on an implementation, but allows the implementation to change without affecting the abstraction.

- **Composite Pattern**

The Composite pattern treats objects as a group or a single object in the same manner. This pattern involves creating a tree-like structure where a group of objects is treated the same way as a single object.

- **Decorator Pattern**

The Decorator pattern adds new functionality to an existing object without changing its structure. This pattern involves a decorator class that wraps an existing class and provides additional functionality without changing the existing class.

- **Facade Pattern**

The Facade pattern provides a simple interface to a complex subsystem. This pattern involves creating a class that provides a simple interface to a complex subsystem.

- **Flyweight Pattern**

The Flyweight pattern conserves memory by sharing large numbers of similar objects. This pattern involves dividing an object into two parts: a state-dependent part and a state-independent part. The state-independent part can be shared among many instances of the object.

- **Proxy Pattern**

The Proxy pattern provides a placeholder for another object to control access to it. This pattern involves creating a proxy class that represents the functionality of another class. The proxy is used to control access to the other class.

3. Behavioral Patterns

Behavioral patterns deal with communication between objects. They describe how objects interact with each other and how they operate together to create complex systems. It provides the communication patterns between objects in a system. The behavioral pattern describes how different objects interact and operate together. The eleven types of behavioral design patterns are as follows:

- **Chain of Responsibility Pattern**

The Chain of Responsibility pattern allows an object to send a request to a chain of objects. This pattern involves a chain of objects, and each object in the chain can either handle the request or pass it on to the next object in the chain.

- **Command Pattern**

The Command pattern creates objects that encapsulate actions and parameters. This pattern involves creating a command interface and a command class. The command class has all the information needed to execute an action.

- **Interpreter Pattern**

The Interpreter pattern is used to convert a certain value to another value. This pattern involves creating an interpreter that can parse and interpret expressions in a language.

- **Iterator Pattern**

The Iterator pattern provides a way to access the elements of an object without exposing its underlying implementation. This pattern involves creating an iterator class that provides a way to access the elements of an object.

- **Mediator Pattern**

The Mediator pattern defines an object that encapsulates the communication between objects. This pattern involves creating a mediator object that encapsulates the communication between objects.

- **Memento Pattern**

The Memento pattern provides a way to restore an object to its previous state. This pattern involves creating a memento object that encapsulates the state of an object.

- **Observer Pattern**

The Observer pattern provides a way to notify objects when a change occurs. This pattern involves creating an observer interface and an observer class. The observer class can register with the subject to receive notifications.

- **State Pattern**

The State pattern allows an object to change its behavior when its internal state changes. This pattern involves creating a state interface and a state class. The state class represents the different states of an object.

- **Strategy Pattern**

The Strategy pattern allows a client to choose an algorithm from a family of algorithms at runtime. This pattern involves creating a strategy interface and multiple strategy classes. The client sets the strategy at runtime.

- **Template Method Pattern**

The Template Method pattern provides a way to define the skeleton of an algorithm in a superclass, but allow subclasses to override specific steps. This pattern involves creating an abstract class that defines the template method, which calls abstract methods that are defined by subclasses.

- **Visitor Pattern**

The Visitor pattern separates an algorithm from an object structure. This pattern involves creating a visitor interface and a visitor class. The visitor class can visit different objects and perform different operations on them.

2.4   What is the Singleton pattern, and when would you use it?

Singleton is a creational design pattern that allows ensuring that only one instance of a class is created, while providing a global point of access to this object.

The Singleton pattern can be useful in several scenarios where you need to ensure that certain objects are created only once within an application, and that these objects are accessible to every part of the application that needs to use them.

Here are a few cases where Singleton pattern can be helpful:

- When you need to maintain a single point of control over a specific resource or service, e.g. a database connection, a thread pool, or a logging service. - When you want to ensure that there is only one instance of a particular object, e.g. a configuration manager, a cache manager, or a registry.

In general, Singleton pattern is a great choice when you have a class that needs to provide a consistent interface across multiple components of the system, and you want to ensure that all of these components use the same instance of the class.

Here's a basic implementation of the Singleton pattern in Java:

```java
public class Singleton {
  private static Singleton instance;

  // private constructor to prevent direct instantiation
  private Singleton() {}

  // global access point to the Singleton instance
  public static Singleton getInstance() {
    if (instance == null) {
      instance = new Singleton();
    }
    return instance;
  }
}
```

In this example, the Singleton class contains a private constructor to prevent direct instantiation, and a static getInstance() method that returns the single instance of the class. The first time the getInstance() method is called, the Singleton object is instantiated and stored in the instance variable. On subsequent calls, the existing Singleton object is returned.

One potential issue with this implementation is that it is not thread-safe, meaning that it could lead to multiple instances of the Singleton being created if multiple threads try to call getInstance() at the same time. To make the pattern thread-safe, the getInstance() method should be synchronized or use double-check locking.

2.5   Can you explain the Factory Method pattern and provide an example of its usage?

The Factory Method pattern is one of the most commonly used design patterns in object-oriented programming. It falls under the category of creational patterns, as it deals with creating objects. The primary goal of the Factory Method pattern is to provide an interface for creating objects, but it leaves the actual instantiation logic to its sub-classes, thereby promoting loose coupling and increased flexibility.

The pattern consists of a Creator, a Product interface, and Concrete Products that implement the Product interface. The Creator class is the one that has the Factory Method, which is responsible for creating objects of the Concrete Products. The Concrete Products are the various objects that we want to create.

Here is an example of the Factory Method pattern in Java:

```java
interface Car { // Product interface
    void drive();
}

class Sedan implements Car { // Concrete Product
    public void drive() {
        System.out.println("Driving a sedan");
    }
}
```

```
class SUV implements Car { // Another Concrete Product
    public void drive() {
        System.out.println("Driving an SUV");
    }
}

abstract class CarFactory { // Creator
    abstract Car createCar();
}

class SedanFactory extends CarFactory { // Concrete Creator
    Car createCar() {
        return new Sedan();
    }
}

class SUVFactory extends CarFactory { // Another Concrete Creator
    Car createCar() {
        return new SUV();
    }
}

public class Main {
    public static void main(String[] args) {
        CarFactory factory = new SedanFactory(); // Creator can be
            switched out for another Concrete Creator at runtime
        Car car = factory.createCar(); // Driver code does not depend
            on Concrete Products, only on creator interface
        car.drive(); // Outputs "Driving a sedan"
    }
}
```

In this example, we have the Product interface 'Car', and two Concrete Products, 'Sedan' and 'SUV'. We also have the Creator abstract class 'CarFactory', which has the Factory Method 'createCar()'. The two Concrete Creators, 'SedanFactory' and 'SUVFactory', inherit from the 'CarFactory' class and implement their own respective 'createCar()' methods, which return instances of their respective Concrete Products.

The Driver code 'Main' creates an instance of 'SedanFactory' as a Creator, but at runtime, it can be switched out for any other Concrete Creator without affecting the logic of 'Main'. We then call the 'createCar()' method on the factory, which returns an instance of a Concrete Product, which we can use without knowing which specific Product was instantiated. Finally, we call the 'drive()' method, which outputs either "Driving a sedan" or "Driving an SUV", depending on which Concrete Product was created.

2.6 What is the Observer pattern, and in which scenarios is it useful?

The Observer pattern is a design pattern that allows an object (known as the subject) to maintain a list of its dependents (known as observers) and notify them automatically of any state changes. This pattern follows the principle of loose coupling, which means that objects are independent of each other and can interact without knowing each other's implementation details. The Observer pattern is also a key component of the Model-View-Controller (MVC) architectural pattern.

In the Observer pattern, the subject object maintains a list of observers and provides methods to add, remove and notify observers. The observers subscribe to the subject and receive notifications automatically when the state of the subject changes. The subject notifies the observers by calling their update() method, which they implement.

The Observer pattern is useful in scenarios where there is a need for multiple objects to be notified automatically when the state of another object changes. For example, consider a stock market application which displays real-time data on stocks. In this scenario, there are multiple objects (e.g. charts, tables, graphs) that need to be updated automatically when the stock price changes. The Observer pattern can be used to implement this

functionality, with the subject being the stock and the observers
being the various display objects.

Here is a Java code example demonstrating the Observer pattern:

```java
import java.util.ArrayList;
import java.util.List;

interface Observer {
    public void update(int value);
}

class Subject {
    private List<Observer> observers;
    private int state;

    public Subject() {
        observers = new ArrayList<>();
    }

    public void add(Observer o) {
        observers.add(o);
    }

    public void remove(Observer o) {
        observers.remove(o);
    }

    public void setState(int value) {
        state = value;
        notifyObservers();
    }

    private void notifyObservers() {
        for (Observer o : observers) {
            o.update(state);
        }
    }
}

class ConcreteObserver1 implements Observer {

    @Override
    public void update(int value) {
        System.out.println("ConcreteObserver1: " + value);
    }
}

class ConcreteObserver2 implements Observer {

    @Override
    public void update(int value) {
```

```
            System.out.println("ConcreteObserver2:␣" + value);
    }
}

public class ObserverExample {
    public static void main(String[] args) {
        Subject subject = new Subject();
        ConcreteObserver1 observer1 = new ConcreteObserver1();
        ConcreteObserver2 observer2 = new ConcreteObserver2();

        // Subscribe observers to subject
        subject.add(observer1);
        subject.add(observer2);

        // Change state of subject and notify observers
        subject.setState(10);

        // Unsubscribe one observer from subject
        subject.remove(observer1);

        // Change state of subject and notify remaining observer
        subject.setState(20);
    }
}
```

In the code example above, the Subject class represents the subject object which maintains a list of observers and notifies them when its state changes. The ConcreteObserver1 and ConcreteObserver2 classes represent the observer objects which implement the Observer interface and provide their own update() method.

In the main method, we create a new Subject object and two ConcreteObserver objects. We subscribe both observers to the subject using the add() method. We change the state of the subject using the setState() method and notify the observers automatically using the notifyObservers() method. We also unsubscribe one observer from the subject using the remove() method and change the state of the subject again to ensure that only the remaining observer is notified.

The output of the code example will be:

```
ConcreteObserver1: 10
ConcreteObserver2: 10
ConcreteObserver2: 20
```

This output confirms that both observers were notified automatically when the state of the subject changed, and only the remaining observer was notified when one of the observers was unsubscribed from the subject.

2.7   Describe the Decorator pattern and give an example of how it can be applied.

The Decorator pattern is a structural design pattern that allows behavior to be added to an individual object, either statically or dynamically, without affecting the behavior of other objects from the same class. The decorator pattern is used when we want to add features to a class, but we don't want to change the current implementation of the class directly.

The Decorator pattern works by extending an object's behavior without changing its implementation. It's usually implemented by creating a Decorator class which wraps the original object and provides additional functionality keeping the signature of the original interface.

A simple example to understand the decorator pattern would be a coffee shop, where customers can choose to add extra ingredients to their coffee, such as milk, sugar, whipped cream or caramel. These extra ingredients can be seen as decorators, where they enhance the original coffee, without changing the espresso itself. The Espresso class is wrapped with a

MilkDecorator, SugarDecorator, WhippedCreamDecorator, or
CaramelDecorator.

Here's an example in Java:

```java
// Component Interface
interface Coffee {
    public double getCost(); // returns the cost of the coffee
    public String getDescription(); // returns the description of the
            coffee
}

// Concrete Component
class Espresso implements Coffee {
    @Override
    public double getCost() {
        return 1.99;
    }
    @Override
    public String getDescription() {
        return "Espresso";
    }
}

// Decorator Class
abstract class CoffeeDecorator implements Coffee {
    protected Coffee decoratedCoffee;
    protected String ingredientSeparator = ",␣";

    public CoffeeDecorator(Coffee decoratedCoffee) {
        this.decoratedCoffee = decoratedCoffee;
    }

    @Override
    public double getCost() { // delegated to concrete components
        return decoratedCoffee.getCost();
    }

    @Override
    public String getDescription() { // delegated to concrete
            components
        return decoratedCoffee.getDescription();
    }
}

// Concrete Decorators
class MilkDecorator extends CoffeeDecorator {
    public MilkDecorator(Coffee decoratedCoffee) {
        super(decoratedCoffee);
    }

    @Override
    public double getCost() {
```

```
        return super.getCost() + 0.20;
    }

    @Override
    public String getDescription() {
        return super.getDescription() + ingredientSeparator + "Milk";
    }
}

class SugarDecorator extends CoffeeDecorator {
    public SugarDecorator(Coffee decoratedCoffee) {
        super(decoratedCoffee);
    }

    @Override
    public double getCost() {
        return super.getCost() + 0.10;
    }

    @Override
    public String getDescription() {
        return super.getDescription() + ingredientSeparator + "Sugar"
            ;
    }
}
```

In this example, we have a 'Coffee' interface, which is implemented by the 'Espresso' class. The 'CoffeeDecorator' class is the abstract decorator and is inherited by 'MilkDecorator' and 'SugarDecorator'. These decorators wrap the original 'Espresso' object and add the ingredients ('Milk' and 'Sugar') to the coffee.

Here's how we can use it:

```
Coffee coffee = new SugarDecorator(new MilkDecorator(new Espresso())
    );
System.out.println(coffee.getCost()); // Output: 2.29
System.out.println(coffee.getDescription()); // Output: Espresso,
    Milk, Sugar
```

In the above example, we can see that we are creating a new 'Coffee' object and wrapping it with two decorators, 'SugarDecorator' and 'MilkDecorator', which adds to the cost of the coffee and the description.

2.8   What is the difference between the Strategy pattern and the State pattern?

Both the Strategy pattern and the State pattern are part of the behavioral design patterns in software design. They both involve dynamically changing the behavior of an object at runtime depending on its internal state.

However, the main difference lies in their intent and implementation.

The Strategy pattern is used to define a family of algorithms, encapsulate each one of them, and make them interchangeable. It allows the algorithm to vary independently from the client that uses it. The pattern consists of four main components:

- Context: the object that needs to change its behavior dynamically.

- Strategy: an interface or abstract class that defines a set of algorithms or behaviors to implement.

- Concrete strategies: a set of concrete classes that implement the strategy or algorithm defined by the Strategy interface.

- Client: the object that creates a Context object and sets a specific strategy for it.

Here is an example of the Strategy pattern in Java:

```java
public interface CompressionStrategy {
  public void compressFile(String fileName);
}

public class ZipCompressionStrategy implements CompressionStrategy {
  public void compressFile(String fileName) {
    System.out.println(fileName + " compressed using zip
        compression");
  }
```

```java
    }

    public class RarCompressionStrategy implements CompressionStrategy {
        public void compressFile(String fileName) {
            System.out.println(fileName + " compressed using rar
                compression");
        }
    }

    public class CompressionContext {
        private CompressionStrategy strategy;

        public void setCompressionStrategy(CompressionStrategy strategy)
            {
            this.strategy = strategy;
        }

        public void createArchive(String fileName) {
            strategy.compressFile(fileName);
        }
    }

    public class Client {
        public static void main(String args[]) {
            CompressionContext ctx = new CompressionContext();
            ctx.setCompressionStrategy(new ZipCompressionStrategy());
            ctx.createArchive("sample.txt");
            ctx.setCompressionStrategy(new RarCompressionStrategy());
            ctx.createArchive("sample.txt");
        }
    }
```

In this example, we have a Context class called Compression-Context, which takes a CompressionStrategy object and uses it to compress files. We have two Concrete strategies: ZipCompressionStrategy and RarCompressionStrategy. The Client creates a CompressionContext object and sets a specific CompressionStrategy for it.

On the other hand, the State pattern is used when an object needs to change its behavior based on its internal state. It allows an object to alter its behavior when its internal state changes. The pattern consists of four main components:

- Context: the object that has an internal state and whose behavior changes based on that state.

- State: an interface or abstract class that defines a set of behaviors for a Context object in a particular state.

- Concrete states: a set of concrete classes that implement the State interface, each with a specific behavior for a particular state.

- Client: the object that creates a Context object and changes its state as necessary.

Here is an example of the State pattern in Java:

```java
public interface State {
   public void doAction(Context context);
}

public class StartState implements State {
   public void doAction(Context context) {
      System.out.println("Player is in start state");
      context.setState(this);
   }

   public String toString(){
      return "Start State";
   }
}

public class StopState implements State {
   public void doAction(Context context) {
      System.out.println("Player is in stop state");
      context.setState(this);
   }

   public String toString(){
      return "Stop State";
   }
}

public class Context {
   private State state;

   public Context(){
      state = null;
   }

   public void setState(State state){
      this.state = state;
   }

   public State getState(){
      return state;
```

```
    }
  }
public class Client {
  public static void main(String[] args) {
    Context context = new Context();

    StartState startState = new StartState();
    startState.doAction(context);

    System.out.println(context.getState().toString());

    StopState stopState = new StopState();
    stopState.doAction(context);

    System.out.println(context.getState().toString());
  }
}
```

In this example, we have a Context class that has an internal state, initially set to null. We have two Concrete states: StartState and StopState, each with a specific behavior for the Context object in that state. The Client creates a Context object and sets a specific State for it.

In summary, the Strategy pattern is used to define a family of interchangeable algorithms, while the State pattern is used to change the behavior of an object based on its internal state.

2.9   Explain the Adapter pattern and provide a real-world example.

The Adapter pattern is a structural design pattern that allows incompatible interfaces to work together. It is used when we have an existing system with a given interface, but the interface doesn't match the one that a client expects. The adapter pattern acts as a bridge between two incompatible interfaces, allowing them to work together.

The adapter pattern consists of three key elements:

- The **Client**: The client is the object that needs to use the incompatible interface.

- The **Adaptee**: The adaptee is the object that provides the incompatible interface.

- The **Adapter**: The adapter is responsible for bridging the gap between the Client and the Adaptee by implementing the interface that the client expects and delegating calls to the Adaptee.

A simple example of the adapter pattern can be seen in a power adapter for international travel. When traveling to a foreign country, the electrical outlet in the hotel room may have a different shape or voltage than what is needed to charge your device. To solve this, you can use a power adapter that plugs into the foreign outlet, and then allows you to plug your device into the adapter. The power adapter acts as an adapter, converting the incompatible interface of the foreign outlet into the compatible interface that your device expects.

Another example of the adapter pattern can be seen in the use of third-party libraries. Suppose we already have an application that uses a specific library for data storage, and the library has a specific interface. However, a new version of the library introduces a new interface, which is not compatible with the existing application. In this case, we can create an adapter to bridge the gap between the old interface and the new one, allowing the application to continue using the old library without requiring any significant changes.

Here is a Java code example of the adapter pattern using the power adapter scenario:

```
// This is the Client
class Phone {
```

```
    private PowerSource powerSource;

    public void setPowerSource(PowerSource powerSource) {
        this.powerSource = powerSource;
    }

    public void charge() {
        int volts = powerSource.getVolts();
        System.out.println("Charging phone with "+volts+" volts");
    }
}

// This is the Adaptee
class ElectricalOutlet {
    public int getVoltage() {
        return 220;
    }
}

// This is the Adapter
class PowerAdapter implements PowerSource {
    private ElectricalOutlet outlet;

    public PowerAdapter(ElectricalOutlet outlet) {
        this.outlet = outlet;
    }

    public int getVolts() {
        int voltage = outlet.getVoltage();
        System.out.println("Converting "+voltage+" volts to 5 volts")
            ;
        return 5;
    }
}

// This is the expected interface for the Client
interface PowerSource {
    int getVolts();
}

// Example usage of the adapter pattern
Phone phone = new Phone();
ElectricalOutlet outlet = new ElectricalOutlet();
PowerSource adapter = new PowerAdapter(outlet);
phone.setPowerSource(adapter);
phone.charge();
```

In the code example above, the Phone class is our client, which
expects an interface that defines a method getVolts(). However,
the ElectricalOutlet class provides a different interface with a
method getVoltage(). To bridge this gap, we create a Power-

Adapter class that implements the PowerSource interface, and its constructor takes an instance of ElectricalOutlet. The get-Volts() method of the PowerAdapter class converts the voltage of the outlet to 5 volts, which is what the phone expects. Finally, we create an instance of the PowerAdapter class and pass it to the Phone object as its power source. The phone can now charge with the power adapter, which acts as an adapter between the incompatible interfaces of the phone and electrical outlet.

2.10 What is the Command pattern, and what are its benefits?

The Command pattern is a behavioral design pattern that converts requests or simple operations into objects. These objects encapsulate the request or operation, allowing you to delay or queue requests, undo/redo actions, and support various forms of program execution. In essence, the Command pattern facilitates the separation of concerns by decoupling the sender and receiver of a command.

The Command pattern has four main components:

1. Command Interface: Declares the method(s) for executing the command.

2. Concrete Command Implementations: Provides the implementation for the Command Interface.

3. Invoker: Takes a command object and is responsible for executing it.

4. Receiver: Performs the actual business logic associated with the command.

Here is an example of the Command pattern implemented in Java:

```java
// Command Interface
public interface Command {
    void execute();
}

// Concrete Command Implementation
public class ConcreteCommand implements Command {
    private Receiver receiver;

    public ConcreteCommand(Receiver recv) {
        this.receiver = recv;
    }

    @Override
    public void execute() {
        receiver.action();
    }
}

// Receiver
public class Receiver {
    public void action() {
        System.out.println("Performing action");
    }
}

// Invoker
public class Invoker {
    private Command command;

    public void setCommand(Command cmd) {
        this.command = cmd;
    }

    public void executeCommand() {
        command.execute();
    }
}

// Client
public class Client {
    public static void main(String[] args) {
        Receiver receiver = new Receiver();
        Command concreteCommand = new ConcreteCommand(receiver);

        Invoker invoker = new Invoker();
        invoker.setCommand(concreteCommand);
        invoker.executeCommand(); // Outputs "Performing action"
    }
}
```

Benefits of the Command pattern:

1. Decouples the sender and receiver of a command, allowing for greater flexibility of requests and operations.

2. Enables the creation of undo/redo functionality by recording a history of commands and reversing their effects.

3. Provides a framework for extensibility and maintainability by allowing for the addition of new commands without affecting the object being acted upon.

4. Supports the construction of complex command hierarchies and composite commands.

2.11   What is the Prototype pattern, and when should you use it?

The Prototype pattern is a creational design pattern that allows an object to create a copy of itself, providing a way to compose new objects from existing ones without exposing their underlying implementation details. The basic idea behind the Prototype pattern is to create new objects by cloning existing ones rather than creating them from scratch, which can be a more efficient way of generating complex objects that require significant processing resources to initialize.

In the Prototype pattern, a prototype interface or abstract class defines the method or methods that can be used to clone the object. Concrete implementations of this interface or abstract class provide the actual implementation details for the cloning operation. When a new object is created, it is created by cloning an existing object through the prototype method.

One of the main benefits of the Prototype pattern is that it allows you to avoid the cost of creating new objects from scratch when you need a large number of similar objects. By copying an existing object, you can save processing time and memory, since you don't need to initialize a new object entirely.

Another advantage of the Prototype pattern is that it allows you to easily create complex objects that are composed of smaller, simpler objects. By creating a prototype for each of the smaller objects, you can use these prototypes to assemble larger, more complex objects without having to define every aspect of their implementation in one place.

In Java, the Prototype pattern can be implemented using the Cloneable interface and the clone() method. The Cloneable interface does not have any methods, but it serves as a marker interface that indicates that the class implementing it can be cloned. The clone() method is defined in the Object class, but it must be overridden in each concrete class that implements the Cloneable interface in order to define the specific cloning behavior for that class. Here's an example of how the Prototype pattern can be implemented in Java using the Cloneable interface:

```
public abstract class Prototype implements Cloneable {
    public abstract Prototype clone();
}

public class ConcretePrototype1 extends Prototype {
    private int field1;

    public ConcretePrototype1(int field1) {
        this.field1 = field1;
    }

    public int getField1() {
        return field1;
    }

    public Prototype clone() {
        return new ConcretePrototype1(this.field1);
    }
}
```

```
public class ConcretePrototype2 extends Prototype {
    private String field2;

    public ConcretePrototype2(String field2) {
        this.field2 = field2;
    }

    public String getField2() {
        return field2;
    }

    public Prototype clone() {
        return new ConcretePrototype2(this.field2);
    }
}
```

In this example, the Prototype abstract class defines a clone()
method that must be implemented by any concrete class that
extends it. Each concrete class (ConcretePrototype1 and Con-
cretePrototype2) implements the clone() method to return a
new instance of itself with the same field values as the original
instance.

To create a new object using a prototype, you would first create
an instance of the existing object that you want to clone, and
then call its clone() method to create a new object. Here's an
example:

```
Prototype original = new ConcretePrototype1(42);
Prototype clone = original.clone();
```

In this example, a new instance of ConcretePrototype1 is created with a value of 42 for the field1 property. Then, the clone()
method is called on the original instance to create a new instance of ConcretePrototype1 with the same field1 value.

2.12   Can you explain the Builder pattern and provide an example of its usage?

The Builder pattern is a creational design pattern that separates the construction of a complex object from its representation, allowing the same construction process to create various representations. It is used when we want to create complex objects that have multiple components, which may or may not be required, in a step-by-step manner. This pattern provides a flexible and reusable way to create and represent different types of objects using the same construction process.

In essence, the Builder pattern involves creating a separate Builder class that takes on the responsibility of constructing the object. The Builder contains methods to populate the required fields and optional fields of the object being built. At the end of the construction process, the Builder returns the finished product.

Here is an example to help illustrate the Builder pattern:

Suppose we want to create a Pizza object that has different toppings. We can use the Builder pattern to create a flexible and modular process for constructing our Pizza objects.

First, we create a PizzaBuilder class that takes on the responsibility of constructing our Pizza object. The PizzaBuilder contains a method for each type of topping we want to include in our Pizza object.

```
public class Pizza {
    private String dough = "";
    private String sauce = "";
    private String cheese = "";
    private List<String> toppings = new ArrayList<>();
```

```java
    public void setDough(String dough) {
        this.dough = dough;
    }

    public void setSauce(String sauce) {
        this.sauce = sauce;
    }

    public void setCheese(String cheese) {
        this.cheese = cheese;
    }

    public void setToppings(List<String> toppings) {
        this.toppings = toppings;
    }

    public String getDescription() {
        StringBuilder sb = new StringBuilder();
        sb.append("Pizza with ").append(this.dough).append(" dough, "
            );
        sb.append(this.sauce).append(" sauce, ").append(this.cheese).
            append(" cheese and toppings: ");
        for (String topping : toppings) {
            sb.append(topping).append(", ");
        }
        sb.setLength(sb.length() - 2);
        return sb.toString();
    }
}

public class PizzaBuilder {
    private Pizza pizza = new Pizza();

    public PizzaBuilder addDough(String dough) {
        pizza.setDough(dough);
        return this;
    }

    public PizzaBuilder addSauce(String sauce) {
        pizza.setSauce(sauce);
        return this;
    }

    public PizzaBuilder addCheese(String cheese) {
        pizza.setCheese(cheese);
        return this;
    }

    public PizzaBuilder addTopping(String topping) {
        pizza.toppings.add(topping);
        return this;
    }

    public Pizza build() {
        return this.pizza;
```

```
    }
  }
```

The Pizza class represents the object we want to construct, and
the PizzaBuilder is responsible for constructing the object. The
Pizza object contains fields for dough type, sauce type, cheese
type, and an arraylist to hold the toppings. We have created
setter methods for each of these fields, which will be used by
the PizzaBuilder to construct the object.

The PizzaBuilder contains setter methods for each of the fields
that we need to set in order to construct our Pizza object. We
have also included a build() method that returns the finished
Pizza object.

Now, we can use the PizzaBuilder to construct our Pizza object,
as shown below:

```
Pizza pizza = new PizzaBuilder()
           .addDough("Thin")
           .addSauce("Tomato")
           .addCheese("Mozzarella")
           .addTopping("Mushrooms")
           .addTopping("Onions")
           .build();

System.out.println(pizza.getDescription());
```

This will create a Pizza object with thin crust, tomato sauce,
Mozzarella cheese, mushrooms, and onions as toppings.

The Builder pattern provides a flexible and modular way to construct complex objects in a step-by-step manner. It separates
the construction of the object from its representation, allowing
different representations to be created using the same construction process. This pattern helps to keep the construction code
clean and maintainable, and it makes it easy to add new components to the object being constructed without changing the

existing code.

2.13 What is the Facade pattern, and how does it simplify complex systems?

The Facade pattern is a software design pattern that provides a simple interface to a complex system or a set of interfaces that together make up a complex system. It is used to hide the complexity of the system and provide a simplified interface to clients.

The Facade pattern provides a single, unified interface to a set of interfaces in a subsystem, making it easier to use. It encapsulates a set of subsystems and provides a simple interface to access them. This makes it easier for clients to use the subsystems without needing to understand the complexities of each subsystem.

The Facade pattern simplifies complex systems in several ways:

- It reduces the complexity by providing a simplified interface.

- It decouples the subsystems from the clients, making the subsystems easier to modify and maintain.

- It promotes code reuse, as the subsystems can be reused in other parts of the system without needing to rewrite the code.

- It improves the system's performance by reducing the number of direct interactions between the clients and subsystems.

A simple example of the Facade pattern can be illustrated with a Banking system. The banking system is composed of different subsystems such as Account, Transaction, and Loan. The

Account subsystem handles account-related operations such as creating an account, withdrawing money, and depositing money. The Transaction subsystem handles transaction-related operations such as transferring money between accounts. The Loan subsystem handles loan-related operations such as approving and disbursing loans. Without using Facade pattern, the client would need to interact with each of these subsystems individually, which would make the system difficult to understand and use. However, using the Facade pattern, a simplified interface can be provided to clients that encapsulates the complexities of each subsystem. In this way, the client need only interact with a single interface to access all the required features of the system.

Here is an example of how the Facade pattern can be implemented in Java:

```java
//Subsystem 1: Account
class Account {
    public void createAccount() {
        System.out.println("Account created.");
    }

    public void depositMoney() {
        System.out.println("Money deposited.");
    }

    public void withdrawMoney() {
        System.out.println("Money withdrawn.");
    }
}

//Subsystem 2: Transaction
class Transaction {
    public void transferMoney() {
        System.out.println("Money transferred.");
    }
}

//Subsystem 3: Loan
class Loan {
    public void approveLoan() {
        System.out.println("Loan approved.");
    }
```

```java
    public void disburseLoan() {
        System.out.println("Loan disbursed.");
    }
}

// Facade class
class BankFacade {
    private Account account;
    private Transaction transaction;
    private Loan loan;

    public BankFacade() {
        account = new Account();
        transaction = new Transaction();
        loan = new Loan();
    }

    public void createAccount() {
        account.createAccount();
    }

    public void depositMoney() {
        account.depositMoney();
    }

    public void withdrawMoney() {
        account.withdrawMoney();
    }

    public void transferMoney() {
        transaction.transferMoney();
    }

    public void approveLoan() {
        loan.approveLoan();
    }

    public void disburseLoan() {
        loan.disburseLoan();
    }
}

// Client code
public class Main {
    public static void main(String[] args) {
        BankFacade bank = new BankFacade();
        bank.createAccount();
        bank.depositMoney();
        bank.withdrawMoney();
        bank.transferMoney();
        bank.approveLoan();
        bank.disburseLoan();
    }
```

```
}
```

In the above example, the BankFacade class provides a simplified interface to the Account, Transaction, and Loan subsystems. The client only needs to interact with the BankFacade
class to perform all the necessary banking operations, while the
BankFacade class handles the complexities of the subsystems.

2.14   Describe the Chain of Responsibil-
ity pattern and give an example of
its application.

The Chain of Responsibility pattern is a behavioral pattern
that allows a set of objects or handlers to handle a request or
message, passing it along to the next object if the current object
cannot handle the request. The idea behind the pattern is to
decouple the sender of the request from the receiver, and allow
multiple objects to handle the request, without knowing which
object will handle the request or how many objects will handle
it.

In a chain of objects, each object has a reference to the next
object in the chain (or null if it is the last object in the chain).
When an object receives a request or message, it can do one of
three things:

1. Handle the request and return a result.

2. Forward the request to the next object in the chain.

3. Do nothing, if the object cannot handle the request and there is
no next object in the chain.

Here's an example of how the Chain of Responsibility pattern can be used to handle requests in a banking system. Suppose a bank has three different types of accounts: Checking, Savings, and Investment. Each account has its own overdraft limit, and when a customer tries to withdraw money, the bank needs to check if the account has sufficient funds. If not, the bank needs to decide if the customer is eligible for an overdraft, based on the overdraft limit of the account.

To implement this functionality using the Chain of Responsibility pattern, we can create three different handlers: CheckingHandler, SavingsHandler, and InvestmentHandler. Each handler in the chain has a reference to the next handler in the chain (or null if it is the last handler in the chain). The CheckingHandler can handle requests related to checking accounts, and if it cannot handle the request, it forwards it to the SavingsHandler. The SavingsHandler can handle requests related to savings accounts, and if it cannot handle the request, it forwards it to the InvestmentHandler. The InvestmentHandler can handle requests related to investment accounts, and if it cannot handle the request, it does nothing.

Here's an example implementation of the three handlers:

Listing 2.1: Handler interface

```
public interface AccountHandler {
    void setNext(AccountHandler handler);
    void withdraw(Account account, double amount);
}
```

Listing 2.2: Checking Handler

```
public class CheckingHandler implements AccountHandler {

    private AccountHandler next;

    @Override
    public void setNext(AccountHandler handler) {
```

```
        this.next = handler;
    }

    @Override
    public void withdraw(Account account, double amount) {
        if (account instanceof CheckingAccount) {
            CheckingAccount checkingAccount = (CheckingAccount)
                account;
            double balance = checkingAccount.getBalance();
            double overdraftLimit = checkingAccount.getOverdraftLimit
                ();
            if (balance + overdraftLimit >= amount) {
                checkingAccount.setBalance(balance - amount);
                System.out.println("Withdrawal of $" + amount + " from
                    Checking Account successful.");
            } else if (next != null) {
                next.withdraw(account, amount);
            } else {
                System.out.println("Withdrawal of $" + amount + " from
                    Checking Account failed. Overdraft limit
                    exceeded.");
            }
        }
    }
}
```

Listing 2.3: Savings Handler

```
public class SavingsHandler implements AccountHandler {

    private AccountHandler next;

    @Override
    public void setNext(AccountHandler handler) {
        this.next = handler;
    }

    @Override
    public void withdraw(Account account, double amount) {
        if (account instanceof SavingsAccount) {
            SavingsAccount savingsAccount = (SavingsAccount) account;
            double balance = savingsAccount.getBalance();
            double overdraftLimit = savingsAccount.getOverdraftLimit()
                ;
            if (balance + overdraftLimit >= amount) {
                savingsAccount.setBalance(balance - amount);
                System.out.println("Withdrawal of $" + amount + " from
                    Savings Account successful.");
            } else if (next != null) {
                next.withdraw(account, amount);
            } else {
                System.out.println("Withdrawal of $" + amount + " from
                    Savings Account failed. Overdraft limit exceeded
```

```
                        .");
             }
         }
     }
 }
```

Listing 2.4: Investment Handler

```
public class InvestmentHandler implements AccountHandler {

    private AccountHandler next;

    @Override
    public void setNext(AccountHandler handler) {
        this.next = handler;
    }

    @Override
    public void withdraw(Account account, double amount) {
        if (account instanceof InvestmentAccount) {
            InvestmentAccount investmentAccount = (InvestmentAccount)
                account;
            double balance = investmentAccount.getBalance();
            double overdraftLimit = investmentAccount.
                getOverdraftLimit();
            if (balance + overdraftLimit >= amount) {
                investmentAccount.setBalance(balance - amount);
                System.out.println("Withdrawal of $" + amount + " from
                    Investment Account successful.");
            } else if (next != null) {
                next.withdraw(account, amount);
            } else {
                System.out.println("Withdrawal of $" + amount + " from
                    Investment Account failed. Overdraft limit
                    exceeded.");
            }
        }
    }
}
```

In this example, the CheckingHandler is the first handler in the chain, followed by the SavingsHandler and the InvestmentHandler. Each handler checks if it can handle the request based on the type of account, and if it cannot handle the request, it forwards it to the next handler in the chain. If there is no next handler in the chain, it prints an error message indicating that the withdrawal failed.

This implementation of the Chain of Responsibility pattern allows for flexible handling of requests in a banking system, and can be easily extended to account for additional types of accounts or different types of requests.

2.15   What is the difference between the Composite pattern and the Flyweight pattern?

The Composite pattern and the Flyweight pattern are both structural design patterns that are used to deal with objects in large quantities. However, they address different aspects of the object structure, and their implementations vary accordingly.

The Composite pattern is used when we need to treat a group of objects in the same manner as a single object. The pattern allows us to compose objects into a tree structure and to work with individual objects and groups of objects uniformly. The key benefit of the Composite pattern is that it enables us to create hierarchical structures with simple components, making them easy to add, remove, or modify. The pattern defines two types of objects, namely the **composite** objects and the **leaf** objects. The composite objects are containers, that is, they contain one or more components (either composite or leaf), whereas the leaf objects are the smallest unit of the composition.

Here is an example of the Composite pattern implemented in Java:

```
public interface Component {
    void operation();
```

```
    }

public class Leaf implements Component {
    @Override
    public void operation() {
        System.out.println("Leaf operation executed");
    }
}

public class Composite implements Component {
    private List<Component> components = new ArrayList<>();

    public void addComponent(Component component) {
        components.add(component);
    }

    public void removeComponent(Component component) {
        components.remove(component);
    }

    @Override
    public void operation() {
        System.out.println("Composite operation executed");
        for (Component component : components) {
            component.operation();
        }
    }
}
```

The Flyweight pattern, on the other hand, is used to minimize memory usage when dealing with large quantities of objects. The pattern is based on the idea of sharing objects that
have similar characteristics, instead of creating new objects each
time. This means that the pattern tries to maximize the number of objects that can be shared (i.e., made into "flyweights"),
while minimizing the number of objects that are unique. The
pattern defines two types of objects, namely the **flyweight**
objects and the **context** objects. The flyweight objects are
the objects that can be shared among multiple context objects,
whereas the context objects are the objects that contain the
unique state of the objects.

Here is an example of the Flyweight pattern implemented in
Java:

```java
public interface Flyweight {
    void operation(Context context);
}

public class ConcreteFlyweight implements Flyweight {
    private final String intrinsicState;

    public ConcreteFlyweight(String intrinsicState) {
        this.intrinsicState = intrinsicState;
    }

    @Override
    public void operation(Context context) {
        System.out.println(String.format("ConcreteFlyweight %s: %s",
            intrinsicState, context.getState()));
    }
}

public class FlyweightFactory {
    private Map<String, Flyweight> flyweights = new HashMap<>();

    public Flyweight getFlyweight(String intrinsicState) {
        if (!flyweights.containsKey(intrinsicState)) {
            flyweights.put(intrinsicState, new ConcreteFlyweight(
                intrinsicState));
        }
        return flyweights.get(intrinsicState);
    }
}

public class Context {
    private final String state;
    private final Flyweight flyweight;

    public Context(String state, Flyweight flyweight) {
        this.state = state;
        this.flyweight = flyweight;
    }

    public String getState() {
        return state;
    }

    public void operation() {
        flyweight.operation(this);
    }
}
```

In summary, the Composite pattern is used to treat a group
of objects in the same manner as an individual object, whereas
the Flyweight pattern is used to minimize memory usage when
dealing with large quantities of objects. The Composite pattern

allows the creation of hierarchical structures of simple components, and the Flyweight pattern enables the sharing of objects that have similar characteristics to minimize the number
of unique objects.

2.16   Can you explain the Mediator pat-
tern and provide a practical example?

Mediator pattern is a behavioral design pattern that allows
loose coupling among objects by controlling communication between them through a mediator object. This pattern defines an
object that encapsulates how a set of objects interact, providing
a centralized control point for communication instead of each
object directly communicating with the others.

The Mediator pattern promotes decoupling by ensuring that
no objects are aware of the logic of the communication between them. Instead, they only communicate with the mediator, which handles the interactions and updates the objects
as needed. This design pattern is useful when the communication logic between objects is complex, and the interaction of the
objects must be tightly controlled to prevent them from being
tightly coupled.

Example: Let's consider an example of a chat application where
multiple users can send and receive messages to/from each other.
In this case, Mediator pattern can be used to simplify the process of managing the communication between users. The mediator object in this case is the chat room, which controls the
communication between users. The users are the objects being

mediated, each with their own send message method.

Here is an example implementation of this pattern:

```java
// Interface for mediator
public interface ChatRoom {
    void send(String message, User sender);
    void addUser(User user);
}

// Concrete mediator
public class ChatRoomImpl implements ChatRoom {
    private List<User> users;

    public ChatRoomImpl() {
        this.users = new ArrayList<>();
    }

    @Override
    public void send(String message, User sender) {
        for (User user : this.users) {
            // Don't send the message back to the sender
            if (!user.equals(sender)) {
                user.receive(message);
            }
        }
    }

    @Override
    public void addUser(User user) {
        this.users.add(user);
    }
}

// Interface for colleagues
public interface User {
    void send(String message);
    void receive(String message);
    void setChatRoom(ChatRoom chatRoom);
}

// Concrete colleague
public class BasicUser implements User {
    private ChatRoom chatRoom;
    private String name;

    public BasicUser(String name) {
        this.name = name;
    }

    @Override
    public void send(String message) {
        this.chatRoom.send(message, this);
```

```
    }

    @Override
    public void receive(String message) {
        System.out.println(this.name + "␣received␣message:␣" +
            message);
    }

    @Override
    public void setChatRoom(ChatRoom chatRoom) {
        this.chatRoom = chatRoom;
        this.chatRoom.addUser(this);
    }
}
// Usage
public class Main {
    public static void main(String[] args) {
        ChatRoom chatRoom = new ChatRoomImpl();

        User user1 = new BasicUser("John");
        User user2 = new BasicUser("Jane");

        user1.setChatRoom(chatRoom);
        user2.setChatRoom(chatRoom);

        // User1 sends a message to user2
        user1.send("Hello␣user2!");
    }
}
```

In this example, the ChatRoom interface is the mediator, which defines the send and addUser methods. The ChatRoomImpl class is the concrete implementation of the mediator, which maintains a list of users and mediates the communication between them.

The User interface is the colleague interface, which defines the send, receive, and setChatRoom methods. The BasicUser class implements the User interface and sends and receives messages through the mediator.

Using the Mediator pattern in this example simplifies the process of managing the communication between users. Without it, the User objects would have to know about each other and communicate directly, which would result in tight coupling and be difficult to maintain as the number of users grows.

2.17   What is the Proxy pattern, and when would you use it?

The Proxy Pattern is a structural design pattern that provides a surrogate to an actual object. The idea behind the pattern is to allow controlling access to the object. A Proxy does the same work as an object, but explicitly handles the calls to methods in that object.

The Proxy Pattern is used when we want to provide controlled access to an object. It is used to provide a surrogate or place-holder for an object to control access to it. The primary work of a Proxy is to forward method calls to the actual object and potentially do something before or after forwarding the call.

A common use case for Proxy is remote object communication. In this scenario, the Proxy behaves as if it were the actual object. The client that interacts with the Proxy is unaware of any communication happening beyond the Proxy. This scenario is also known as a Remote Proxy.

Another use case is virtual proxy for objects that are expensive to instantiate. When it is costly to create actual objects or load the objects, a Proxy can be a representation of the actual object that loads the actual object when necessary. An example could be loading large images on demand.

A third use case is a protection proxy. In this scenario, the Proxy is used for enforcement of security policies. A protection

Proxy ensures that the client follows the security regulations
before they can use the actual object. An example could be
to restrict the access to sensitive documents in a company by
checking the access level of the user before granting access to
documents.

A Java code example for the Proxy pattern using Remote Proxy
would look like this:

```java
//Interface for remote service
public interface RemoteService {
  public void performOperation();
}

//Service implementation class
public class RemoteServiceImpl implements RemoteService {
  @Override
  public void performOperation() {
    System.out.println("Performing operation...");
  }
}

//Remote Proxy class
public class RemoteProxy implements RemoteService {
  private RemoteService remoteService;

  public RemoteProxy() {
    remoteService = new RemoteServiceImpl(); // Actual object
        inside the proxy
  }

  @Override
  public void performOperation() {
    //Additional control can be added before and after delegating
        the request.
    remoteService.performOperation();
  }
}

//Client code
public class Client {
  public static void main(String[] args) {
    RemoteService object = new RemoteProxy();
    object.performOperation(); //performing operation...
  }
}
```

In this example, the Remote Proxy takes care of delegating to an actual object, 'RemoteServiceImpl' in this case, and provides additional functionality, like extra security checks or remote communication for the client unaware of the communication happening beyond the Proxy.

2.18   Describe the Bridge pattern and provide a real-world example of its usage.

The Bridge pattern is a structural design pattern that separates an abstraction from its implementation so that both can be modified independently. It is used when an abstraction has multiple implementations and the client should be able to switch from one implementation to another without changing the code. The Bridge pattern consists of two main parts: Abstraction and Implementation. Abstraction defines the interface that the client uses and Implementation provides the actual implementation that Abstraction delegates its requests to.

Here's an example to illustrate the Bridge pattern:

Suppose we need to design a drawing tool that can draw different shapes such as circles, squares, and triangles. We'll use the Bridge pattern to separate the abstraction (the drawing tool) from its implementation (the different shapes).

First, we define the Abstraction, which is the drawing tool interface that the client uses:

```
public interface DrawingTool {
    void drawShape();
}
```

Next, we define the Implementation, which is the different shapes
that the drawing tool can draw:

```java
public interface Shape {
    void draw();
}

public class Circle implements Shape {
    @Override
    public void draw() {
        System.out.println("Drawing Circle");
    }
}

public class Square implements Shape {
    @Override
    public void draw() {
        System.out.println("Drawing Square");
    }
}

public class Triangle implements Shape {
    @Override
    public void draw() {
        System.out.println("Drawing Triangle");
    }
}
```

Now, we create a concrete Abstraction class that uses the Implementation:

```java
public class ConcreteDrawingTool implements DrawingTool {
    private final Shape shape;

    public ConcreteDrawingTool(Shape shape) {
        this.shape = shape;
    }

    @Override
    public void drawShape() {
        shape.draw();
    }
}
```

Finally, we create a client that uses the drawing tool to draw
different shapes:

```java
public class Client {
    public static void main(String[] args) {
```

```
DrawingTool circleDrawingTool = new ConcreteDrawingTool(new
    Circle());
DrawingTool squareDrawingTool = new ConcreteDrawingTool(new
    Square());
DrawingTool triangleDrawingTool = new ConcreteDrawingTool(new
    Triangle());

circleDrawingTool.drawShape();
squareDrawingTool.drawShape();
triangleDrawingTool.drawShape();
    }
}
```

In the example above, we used the Bridge pattern to separate the abstraction (DrawingTool) from its implementation (Shape). The client (Client) only interacts with the abstraction and can switch between different implementations (shapes) without changing any code.

2.19 What is the Template Method pattern, and how does it encourage code reusability?

The Template Method pattern is a behavioral design pattern that defines a skeleton of an algorithm in a base class, but lets subclasses override specific steps of the algorithm without changing its structure. The idea behind this pattern is to define a template containing the steps of a certain algorithm, then let the subclasses customize some of those steps as needed, without modifying the overall algorithm structure. In other words, the template method pattern defines an algorithm at a high level, but allows variations at the low level.

The template method pattern is useful when you want to implement an algorithm once, but allow for some parts of it to be customized by subclasses. This can help avoid duplication of code and increase code reusability. By providing a standard implementation of the algorithm and allowing customization of specific steps, subclasses can focus on adding or modifying functionality in a consistent manner.

To implement the template method pattern, we first declare an abstract class that defines the structure of the algorithm. Within this class, we define the template method that contains the overall algorithm structure, calling on other methods which can be overridden by subclasses. These methods are called "hooks" because they provide points where the algorithm can be customized. The subclasses then implement these hooks to provide their own functionality, while leaving the rest of the algorithm intact.

Here is an example implementation in Java:

```java
public abstract class AlgorithmTemplate {

    public void executeAlgorithm() {
        step1();
        step2();
        step3();
    }

    protected abstract void step1();

    protected void step2() {
        // default implementation
    }

    protected abstract void step3();
}
public class SubAlgorithm extends AlgorithmTemplate {

    protected void step1() {
        System.out.println("Step 1 of SubAlgorithm");
    }

    protected void step3() {
        System.out.println("Step 3 of SubAlgorithm");
    }
```

```java
}

public class AnotherSubAlgorithm extends AlgorithmTemplate {

    protected void step1() {
        System.out.println("Step 1 of AnotherSubAlgorithm");
    }

    protected void step2() {
        System.out.println("Custom Step 2 of AnotherSubAlgorithm");
    }

    protected void step3() {
        System.out.println("Step 3 of AnotherSubAlgorithm");
    }
}

// Usage:
AlgorithmTemplate algorithm = new SubAlgorithm();
algorithm.executeAlgorithm();

AlgorithmTemplate anotherAlgorithm = new AnotherSubAlgorithm();
anotherAlgorithm.executeAlgorithm();
```

In this implementation, the 'AlgorithmTemplate' class defines the overall algorithm structure with the 'executeAlgorithm()' method. This method calls on the 'step1()', 'step2()', and 'step3()' methods, which are defined as "hooks" that can be overridden by subclasses. The 'SubAlgorithm' and 'AnotherSubAlgorithm' classes then implement these hooks to provide their own functionality.

By using the template method pattern, we can define a standard algorithm structure in the 'AlgorithmTemplate' class, while allowing for customization in the subclasses. This can make our code more modular and maintainable, enabling us to reuse the same algorithm in different contexts.

2.20   Can you explain the difference between the Abstract Factory pattern and the Factory Method pattern?

Both of these design patterns belong to the category of creational patterns, meaning they are used to provide object creation mechanisms which increase flexibility and reuse of existing code.

Factory Method pattern

The Factory Method pattern is a creational pattern that defines an interface for creating an object, but allows subclasses to choose which class to instantiate. It provides a way for a class to delegate the instantiation of objects to subclasses.

In the Factory Method pattern, we define a factory method in an interface or an abstract class, which returns an object of a different class. The implementation of the factory method can be overridden in the subclass, which decides the specific class for object instantiation.

Here is an example of the Factory Method pattern in Java:

```java
// A product interface
interface Product {
    void use();
}

// Concrete products
class ConcreteProduct1 implements Product {
    @Override
    public void use() {
        System.out.println("Using ConcreteProduct1");
    }
}

class ConcreteProduct2 implements Product {
    @Override
```

```java
    public void use() {
        System.out.println("Using␣ConcreteProduct2");
    }
}

// Abstract creator
abstract class Creator {
    public void someOperation() {
        Product product = createProduct();
        product.use();
    }

    protected abstract Product createProduct();
}

// Concrete creators
class ConcreteCreator1 extends Creator {
    @Override
    protected Product createProduct() {
        return new ConcreteProduct1();
    }
}

class ConcreteCreator2 extends Creator {
    @Override
    protected Product createProduct() {
        return new ConcreteProduct2();
    }
}

// Usage
public class FactoryMethodDemo {
    public static void main(String[] args) {
        Creator creator1 = new ConcreteCreator1();
        creator1.someOperation();

        Creator creator2 = new ConcreteCreator2();
        creator2.someOperation();
    }
}
```

In this example, we have a 'Product' interface and two concrete implementation classes, 'ConcreteProduct1' and 'ConcreteProduct2'. We also have an abstract 'Creator' class which defines the factory method 'createProduct()' and the method 'someOperation()'. The concrete creator classes 'ConcreteCreator1' and 'ConcreteCreator2' override the 'createProduct()' method to return an instance of the corresponding 'ConcreteProduct'.

Abstract Factory pattern

The Abstract Factory pattern is also a creational pattern, which provides an interface for creating families of related or dependent objects, without specifying their concrete classes. It enables the creation of objects that are from the same family or group, which have some similarities and interdependencies.

In the Abstract Factory pattern, the client code does not specify which concrete implementation to use, instead it calls methods from the abstract factory interface to create the family of related objects. The implementation of these methods is provided by the concrete factory classes that implement the abstract factory interface.

Here is an example of the Abstract Factory pattern in Java:

```java
// Abstract product A
interface AbstractProductA {
    void use();
}

// Concrete product A1
class ConcreteProductA1 implements AbstractProductA {
    @Override
    public void use() {
        System.out.println("Using ConcreteProductA1");
    }
}

// Concrete product A2
class ConcreteProductA2 implements AbstractProductA {
    @Override
    public void use() {
        System.out.println("Using ConcreteProductA2");
    }
}

// Abstract product B
interface AbstractProductB {
    void interact(AbstractProductA a);
}

// Concrete product B1
class ConcreteProductB1 implements AbstractProductB {
```

```java
    @Override
    public void interact(AbstractProductA a) {
        System.out.println("Interacting with ConcreteProductA1");
        a.use();
    }
}

// Concrete product B2
class ConcreteProductB2 implements AbstractProductB {
    @Override
    public void interact(AbstractProductA a) {
        System.out.println("Interacting with ConcreteProductA2");
        a.use();
    }
}

// Abstract factory
interface AbstractFactory {
    AbstractProductA createProductA();
    AbstractProductB createProductB();
}

// Concrete factory 1
class ConcreteFactory1 implements AbstractFactory {
    @Override
    public AbstractProductA createProductA() {
        return new ConcreteProductA1();
    }

    @Override
    public AbstractProductB createProductB() {
        return new ConcreteProductB1();
    }
}

// Concrete factory 2
class ConcreteFactory2 implements AbstractFactory {
    @Override
    public AbstractProductA createProductA() {
        return new ConcreteProductA2();
    }

    @Override
    public AbstractProductB createProductB() {
        return new ConcreteProductB2();
    }
}

// Usage
public class AbstractFactoryDemo {
    public static void main(String[] args) {
        AbstractFactory factory1 = new ConcreteFactory1();
        AbstractProductA productA1 = factory1.createProductA();
        AbstractProductB productB1 = factory1.createProductB();
```

```
    productB1.interact(productA1);

    AbstractFactory factory2 = new ConcreteFactory2();
    AbstractProductA productA2 = factory2.createProductA();
    AbstractProductB productB2 = factory2.createProductB();

    productB2.interact(productA2);
  }
}
```

In this example, we have two abstract product interfaces 'AbstractProductA' and 'AbstractProductB' and four concrete product classes 'ConcreteProductA1', 'ConcreteProductA2', 'ConcreteProductB1', and 'ConcreteProductB2'. We also have an abstract factory interface 'AbstractFactory' with two factory methods 'createProductA()' and 'createProductB()'. The concrete factory classes 'ConcreteFactory1' and 'ConcreteFactory2' implement the factory methods to return instances of the corresponding concrete product classes.

Differences

So, to summarize the differences between the Factory Method and Abstract Factory patterns:

- Factory Method creates a single product, while Abstract Factory creates multiple related products.

- Factory Method uses inheritance to delegate instantiation to subclasses, while Abstract Factory uses composition to delegate instantiation to another object.

- Factory Method provides a way to encapsulate a specific algorithm for object creation, while Abstract Factory provides a way to encapsulate object creation for a group of related products.

Chapter 3

Intermediate

3.1 How does the Double-Checked Locking technique work in implementing a thread-safe Singleton pattern?

The Singleton pattern is a design pattern that restricts the instantiation of a class to one object, ensuring that there is only one instance of the class in the entire application. This pattern is often used in situations where a single object needs to coordinate actions across a system. The implementation of Singleton pattern should be thread-safe to ensure that only one instance of the Singleton class is created in a multi-threaded environment.

The Double-Checked Locking technique is one of the thread-safe mechanisms to implement Singleton pattern. This technique is used to reduce the overhead of acquiring a lock every time the

Singleton instance is accessed by the application. The double-checked locking technique involves the following steps:

1. Create a **private** constructor to restrict the instantiation of the Singleton **class**.
2. Create a **private static volatile** variable to hold the Singleton instance. The keyword "volatile" ensures that multiple threads handle the instance variable correctly when it is being initialized to the Singleton instance.
3. Create a **public static** method to provide a global access point to the Singleton instance. In **this** method, we first check **if** the Singleton instance has already been instantiated. If not, then we synchronize on the Singleton class object and check **if** the Singleton instance is still null. If the Singleton instance is null, we create a **new** instance of the Singleton **class** and assign it to the instance variable. Since we are using double-checked locking, we check the instance variable again inside the **synchronized** block to ensure that it is still **null** before creating a **new** instance. After the Singleton instance is created, we release the lock and **return** the Singleton instance to the caller.

Here's an example implementation of the Singleton class using the Double-Checked Locking technique in Java:

```java
public class Singleton {
    private static volatile Singleton instance;

    private Singleton() {
        // Private constructor to restrict instantiation
    }

    public static Singleton getInstance() {
        if (instance == null) {
            synchronized (Singleton.class) {
                if (instance == null) {
                    instance = new Singleton();
                }
            }
        }
        return instance;
    }
}
```

In the code above, the private constructor ensures that the Singleton class cannot be instantiated outside of the class itself. The instance variable is declared as "volatile" to ensure that multiple threads handle it correctly during initialization. The getInstance() method first checks if the instance variable is null

before entering the synchronized block. If the instance variable is null, then the method enters the synchronized block and
checks the instance variable again. If the instance variable is
still null, the method creates a new instance of the Singleton
class and assigns it to the instance variable. Finally, the method
releases the lock and returns the Singleton instance to the caller.

The Double-Checked Locking technique is an effective way to
implement a thread-safe Singleton pattern while minimizing the
overhead of acquiring locks every time the Singleton instance is
accessed. However, it is important to note that prior to Java 5,
it was possible for the instance variable to be non-null before it
was fully initialized, resulting in race conditions. As of Java 5,
this issue has been resolved by adding the "volatile" keyword
to the instance variable declaration.

3.2 Explain the benefits of using the Dependency Inversion Principle with the Factory Method pattern.

The Dependency Inversion Principle (DIP) and the Factory
Method pattern are two important concepts in object-oriented
software design. The DIP states that high-level modules should
not depend on low-level modules, but both should depend on
abstractions. The Factory Method pattern, on the other hand,
provides an interface for creating objects but allows subclasses
to decide which class to instantiate.

When combined, these two patterns can lead to more flexible,
maintainable, and testable code. Here are some of the benefits
of using the DIP with the Factory Method pattern:

1. Decoupling: By using abstractions and interfaces, the high-level modules are decoupled from the low-level modules. This means that changes to the low-level module will not affect the high-level module, and vice versa.

2. Extensibility: The Factory Method pattern makes it easy to add new types of objects to the system. The new objects can be created by adding a new subclass of the factory or by modifying an existing subclass. Since the high-level module only depends on the abstract factory interface, it does not need to be modified.

3. Testability: Because the high-level module only depends on the abstract factory interface, it can be easily tested with a mock or stub factory. This allows for more comprehensive testing of the high-level module, without needing to test the low-level modules.

Here is an example that demonstrates the use of the DIP with the Factory Method pattern in Java:

First, we define an abstract factory interface that will be implemented by the concrete factories:

```
public interface AnimalFactory {
    public Animal createAnimal();
}
```

Next, we define the concrete factories that will create different types of animals:

```
public class CatFactory implements AnimalFactory {
    public Animal createAnimal() {
        return new Cat();
    }
}

public class DogFactory implements AnimalFactory {
```

```
    public Animal createAnimal() {
        return new Dog();
    }
}
```

Finally, we define a high-level module that depends on the abstract factory interface:

```
public class AnimalShelter {
    private AnimalFactory animalFactory;

    public AnimalShelter(AnimalFactory animalFactory) {
        this.animalFactory = animalFactory;
    }

    public void addAnimal() {
        Animal animal = animalFactory.createAnimal();
        // add animal to shelter
    }
}
```

With this design, the AnimalShelter class depends only on the AnimalFactory interface, which is an abstraction that can be implemented by any concrete factory. This allows for easy extensibility and testability of the AnimalShelter class.

3.3 What is the difference between the Observer pattern and the Event Aggregator pattern?

Both the Observer and the Event Aggregator patterns are used to handle communication between different parts of a software system. However, they differ in the way they handle this communication.

The Observer pattern is used when there is a one-to-many relationship between objects, where the state of one object (the

subject) affects the state of many other objects (the observers).
The subject maintains a list of observers and notifies them when
its state changes, so that they can update their own state accordingly. This pattern can be implemented in Java using the
built-in 'Observer' and 'Observable' interfaces.

Here is an example implementation of the Observer pattern in
Java:

```java
import java.util.Observable;
import java.util.Observer;

public class Subject extends Observable {
    private int state;

    public void setState(int state) {
        this.state = state;
        setChanged();
        notifyObservers();
    }

    public int getState() {
        return state;
    }
}

public class ObserverImpl implements Observer {
    @Override
    public void update(Observable o, Object arg) {
        if (o instanceof Subject) {
            Subject subject = (Subject) o;
            int state = subject.getState();
            // Update observer's state based on subject's state
        }
    }
}
```

On the other hand, the Event Aggregator pattern is used to
handle communication between many-to-many relationships. In
this pattern, an event aggregator object collects events from
many sources and notifies many listeners about them. The
listeners subscribe to the aggregator for the events they are interested in, and the aggregator keeps track of them. When an
event is published, the aggregator notifies all the subscribed lis-

teners. This pattern can be implemented in Java using event listeners and dispatchers.

Here is an example implementation of the Event Aggregator pattern in Java:

```java
import java.util.ArrayList;
import java.util.HashMap;
import java.util.List;
import java.util.Map;

public class EventAggregator {
    private Map<String, List<EventListener>> listenersMap = new
        HashMap<>();

    public void subscribe(String eventType, EventListener listener)
        {
        List<EventListener> listeners = listenersMap.get(eventType);
        if (listeners == null) {
            listeners = new ArrayList<>();
            listenersMap.put(eventType, listeners);
        }
        listeners.add(listener);
    }

    public void unsubscribe(String eventType, EventListener listener
        ) {
        List<EventListener> listeners = listenersMap.get(eventType);
        if (listeners != null) {
            listeners.remove(listener);
        }
    }

    public void publish(String eventType) {
        List<EventListener> listeners = listenersMap.get(eventType);
        if (listeners != null) {
            for (EventListener listener : listeners) {
                listener.onEvent(eventType);
            }
        }
    }
}

public interface EventListener {
    void onEvent(String eventType);
}

public class ListenerImpl implements EventListener {
    @Override
    public void onEvent(String eventType) {
        // Handle event
```

```
    }
  }
```

In summary, the Observer pattern is used for one-to-many communication, whereas the Event Aggregator pattern is used for many-to-many communication. Both patterns are useful in different scenarios and can be implemented effectively in Java.

3.4   Can you discuss the advantages of using the Decorator pattern over subclassing when adding responsibilities to objects dynamically?

The Decorator pattern and classic inheritance (sub-classing) are both object-oriented design strategies for extending the functionality of an object. However, they differ in several aspects, such as extensibility, flexibility, and maintenance. In this answer, I will discuss the advantages of using the Decorator pattern over subclassing when adding responsibilities to objects dynamically.

First, the Decorator pattern offers greater flexibility and extensibility compared to inheritance. Inheritance requires creating a new subclass every time a new behavior or responsibility needs to be added to an object. This can result in a large number of classes, which can be difficult to manage and can have performance implications.

In contrast, the Decorator pattern allows developers to add new responsibilities to an object by wrapping it with one or more decorator objects, each providing additional behaviors or responsibilities to the original object. This approach offers a more flexible and scalable solution, as decorators can be added and removed at runtime, without affecting the original object or other decorators.

Here's an example of how the Decorator pattern can be used to add new responsibilities dynamically:

```java
public interface Component {
    void operation();
}

public class ConcreteComponent implements Component {
    public void operation() {
        System.out.println("ConcreteComponent operation.");
    }
}

public abstract class Decorator implements Component {
    private Component component;

    public Decorator(Component component) {
        this.component = component;
    }

    public void operation() {
        component.operation();
    }
}

public class ConcreteDecoratorA extends Decorator {
    public ConcreteDecoratorA(Component component) {
        super(component);
    }

    public void operation() {
        super.operation();
        System.out.println("ConcreteDecoratorA operation.");
    }
}

public class ConcreteDecoratorB extends Decorator {
    public ConcreteDecoratorB(Component component) {
        super(component);
    }

    public void operation() {
        super.operation();
        System.out.println("ConcreteDecoratorB operation.");
    }
```

```
    }
public class Client {
    public static void main(String[] args) {
        Component component = new ConcreteComponent();
        component = new ConcreteDecoratorA(component);
        component = new ConcreteDecoratorB(component);
        component.operation();
    }
}
```

In this example, we have a 'Component' interface and a 'Con-creteComponent' class implementing it. We also have an abstract 'Decorator' class that also implements the 'Component' interface and a 'super()' constructor that takes a 'Component' parameter. The 'ConcreteDecoratorA' and 'ConcreteDecoratorB' classes extend the 'Decorator' class and provide additional behaviors.

In the 'Client' class, we create a 'ConcreteComponent' object and pass it to both 'ConcreteDecoratorA' and 'ConcreteDecoratorB' objects. When we call 'component.operation()', it will execute the 'operation()' method of the 'ConcreteComponent' object followed by the 'operation()' methods of the 'ConcreteDecoratorA' and 'ConcreteDecoratorB' objects.

This approach allows us to add additional behaviors dynamically to the 'Component' object at runtime. We can add as many decorators as we want, and we can even remove them if we no longer need them.

Another advantage of the Decorator pattern is that it promotes code reuse. Decorators can be shared among different objects, and each object can have a unique combination of decorators, providing a more customized and flexible solution.

In conclusion, the Decorator pattern offers several advantages over inheritance when adding responsibilities to objects dynamically. It provides greater flexibility, extensibility, and code reuse, and it allows developers to add new behaviors or responsibilities to an object without modifying the object's class.

3.5 How can you use the Strategy pattern together with the Open/Closed Principle to create flexible and extensible systems?

The Strategy pattern is a behavioral design pattern that enables an object, called the context, to vary its behavior by delegating it to a family of algorithms, called strategies. These algorithms are interchangeable and can be switched at runtime. The Open/Closed Principle (OCP) is a principle in object-oriented design that states that software entities should be open for extension but closed for modification.

Combining the Strategy pattern with the Open/Closed Principle results in flexible and extensible systems because new strategies can be added without modifying the existing codebase, thereby avoiding the risk of introducing new errors or breaking existing code. Furthermore, this approach allows for the creation of new behaviors without recompiling the context or other clients that use it.

To implement this, we start by creating an interface, called the strategy interface or strategy family, that defines the common behavior expected of all strategies. Each strategy then implements this interface and provides its own implementation of the behavior. The context delegates the behavior to a strategy object, which means that the context can use any strategy object, which means that the context can use any strategy object that conforms to the strategy interface. New strategies can be added without modifying the existing codebase by simply creating a new class that implements the strategy interface.

Java code example:

```java
public interface Strategy {
    void doSomething();
}

public class ConcreteStrategy1 implements Strategy {
    @Override
    public void doSomething() {
        //logic for strategy 1
    }
}

public class ConcreteStrategy2 implements Strategy {
    @Override
    public void doSomething() {
        //logic for strategy 2
    }
}

public class Context {
    private Strategy strategy;

    public Context(Strategy strategy) {
        this.strategy = strategy;
    }

    public void setStrategy(Strategy strategy) {
        this.strategy = strategy;
    }

    public void doSomething() {
        strategy.doSomething();
    }
}
```

In the above code, we have defined the strategy interface, 'Strategy'. Two concrete strategies, 'ConcreteStrategy1' and 'ConcreteStrategy2', are also defined. The 'Context' class takes a strategy object in its constructor and delegates behavior to it.

To add a new strategy, all we need to do is create a new class that implements the 'Strategy' interface and provides its own implementation of the behavior. The 'Context' class does not need to be modified to accommodate this new strategy, as long as it conforms to the 'Strategy' interface.

This approach adheres to the Open/Closed Principle because new strategies can be added without modifying existing code. It also provides flexibility and extensibility because the 'Context' class can use any strategy object that conforms to the 'Strategy' interface, which means that new behaviors can be added without recompiling the 'Context' or other clients that use it.

3.6 Explain how the Memento pattern can be used in conjunction with the State pattern to store and restore object states.

The Memento pattern and State pattern are both behavioral design patterns, and they can be used together to implement a solution that manages the states of an object and provides the ability to undo/revert to a previous state.

The State pattern allows an object to alter its behavior when its internal state changes. This pattern encapsulates the object's behavior into separate state objects, which can be changed at runtime based on the state transition. The State pattern ensures that the object's change in behavior is inverted on state change.

On the other hand, the Memento pattern provides the ability

to capture and restore an object's internal state at a particular point in time without breaking encapsulation.

To use these patterns together, we can introduce a Memento object that stores the state of the Subject object. This Memento object will be managed by the Caretaker object, which is responsible for storing and restoring Memento objects. So, when the Subject object changes its state, the State pattern will manage the transition between different states while the Memento pattern will capture the current state of the Subject object and store it in a Memento object.

Here is an example of how this can be implemented:

```java
// Memento class
public class Memento {
  private State state;

  public Memento(State state) {
    this.state = state.clone();
  }

  public State getState() {
    return state;
  }
}

// Caretaker class
public class Caretaker {
  private Stack<Memento> mementos = new Stack<>();

  public void save(Memento memento) {
    mementos.push(memento);
  }

  public Memento restore() {
    if(mementos.empty()) {
      return null;
    }
    return mementos.pop();
  }
}

// Subject class
public class Subject {
  private State state;
```

```java
  public void setState(State state) {
    this.state = state;
  }

  public Memento captureState() {
    return new Memento(state);
  }

  public void restoreState(Memento memento) {
    this.state = memento.getState();
  }
}

// State interface
public interface State {
  void handle();
  State clone();
}

// Concrete State classes
public class StateA implements State {
  private Subject subject;

  public StateA(Subject subject) {
    this.subject = subject;
  }

  @Override
  public void handle() {
    // handle StateA's operation
    subject.setState(new StateB(subject));
  }

  @Override
  public State clone() {
    return new StateA(subject);
  }
}

public class StateB implements State {
  private Subject subject;

  public StateB(Subject subject) {
    this.subject = subject;
  }

  @Override
  public void handle() {
    // handle StateB's operation
    subject.setState(new StateC(subject));
  }

  @Override
  public State clone() {
    return new StateB(subject);
```

```
    }
  }
public class StateC implements State {
  private Subject subject;

  public StateC(Subject subject) {
    this.subject = subject;
  }

  @Override
  public void handle() {
    // handle StateC's operation
  }

  @Override
  public State clone() {
    return new StateC(subject);
  }
}
```

In this example, the 'Subject' class has a 'captureState()' method to capture its internal state and return a 'Memento' object. Similarly, it has a 'restoreState(Memento memento)' method to restore the internal state from a given 'Memento' object.

The 'Caretaker' class manages the stack of 'Memento' objects and provides the ability to store and restore the 'Subject's internal state.

The 'State' interface defines the contract for concrete state classes. Each concrete state class (e.g. 'StateA', 'StateB', and 'StateC') implements the 'State' interface and provides its own implementation for 'handle()' method to perform its specific operations. Additionally, each concrete state class must also implement the clone method to make sure that the behavior change in the class is properly inverted.

In conclusion, the combination of the Memento and State patterns provides a powerful mechanism to store and restore an object's internal state while providing the ability to change the object's behavior based on its current state.

3.7   When should you choose the Adapter pattern over the Facade pattern, and vice versa?

Both the Adapter pattern and Facade pattern are used to simplify the interface of existing classes or subsystems.

The Adapter pattern is used when we have an existing class that provides an interface that is different from the one we need. We use an Adapter to wrap the existing class and provide the interface that our client code needs. The Adapter has a reference to the existing class and translates the client's requests into calls to the appropriate methods on the existing class. In other words, the Adapter pattern is used to make two incompatible interfaces compatible with each other.

On the other hand, the Facade pattern is used when we have a complex subsystem that we want to simplify for our client code. We create a Facade object that provides a simplified interface to the client code. The Facade object delegates the client's requests to the appropriate classes in the subsystem. In other words, the Facade pattern is used to provide a unified interface to a set of interfaces in a subsystem, thus simplifying its usage.

So, when choosing between the Adapter pattern and Facade pattern, we need to consider the following:

1. If we have an existing class that we want to reuse, but its interface is incompatible with our client code, then we should

use the Adapter pattern.

2. If we have a complex subsystem with multiple interfaces and
we want to simplify its usage for our client code, then we should
use the Facade pattern.

Here is an example of how the Adapter pattern can be used in
Java:

```java
public interface MediaPlayer {
  public void play(String audioType, String fileName);
}

public interface AdvancedMediaPlayer {
  public void playVlc(String fileName);
  public void playMp4(String fileName);
}

public class VlcPlayer implements AdvancedMediaPlayer{
  public void playVlc(String fileName) {
    System.out.println("Playing vlc file. Name: "+ fileName);
  }

  public void playMp4(String fileName) {
    // do nothing
  }
}

public class Mp4Player implements AdvancedMediaPlayer{

  public void playVlc(String fileName) {
    // do nothing
  }

  public void playMp4(String fileName) {
    System.out.println("Playing mp4 file. Name: "+ fileName);
  }
}

public class MediaAdapter implements MediaPlayer {

  AdvancedMediaPlayer advancedMusicPlayer;

  public MediaAdapter(String audioType){
    if(audioType.equalsIgnoreCase("vlc") ){
      advancedMusicPlayer = new VlcPlayer();
    } else if (audioType.equalsIgnoreCase("mp4")){
      advancedMusicPlayer = new Mp4Player();
    }
  }
```

```
    public void play(String audioType, String fileName) {

       if(audioType.equalsIgnoreCase("vlc")){
          advancedMusicPlayer.playVlc(fileName);
       }
       else if(audioType.equalsIgnoreCase("mp4")){
          advancedMusicPlayer.playMp4(fileName);
       }
    }
}

public class AudioPlayer implements MediaPlayer {
    MediaAdapter mediaAdapter;

    public void play(String audioType, String fileName) {

       if(audioType.equalsIgnoreCase("mp3")){
          System.out.println("Playing mp3 file. Name: " + fileName);
       }
       else if(audioType.equalsIgnoreCase("vlc") ||
          audioType.equalsIgnoreCase("mp4")){
          mediaAdapter = new MediaAdapter(audioType);
          mediaAdapter.play(audioType, fileName);
       }
       else{
          System.out.println("Invalid media. "+ audioType + " format
                not supported");
       }
    }
}

public class AdapterPatternDemo {
    public static void main(String[] args) {
       AudioPlayer audioPlayer = new AudioPlayer();

       audioPlayer.play("mp3", "beyond_the_horizon.mp3");
       audioPlayer.play("mp4", "alone.mp4");
       audioPlayer.play("vlc", "far_far_away.vlc");
       audioPlayer.play("avi", "mind_me.avi");
    }
}
```

In the above example, we have an AudioPlayer that can play mp3 files natively. However, if it receives a request to play a file of type vlc or mp4, it uses the MediaAdapter to convert the request to a format that it can handle natively.

Here is an example of how the Facade pattern can be used in

Java:

```java
public interface Shape {
   void draw();
}

public class Rectangle implements Shape {

   public void draw() {
      System.out.println("Rectangle::draw()");
   }
}

public class Square implements Shape {

   public void draw() {
      System.out.println("Square::draw()");
   }
}

public class Circle implements Shape {

   public void draw() {
      System.out.println("Circle::draw()");
   }
}

public class ShapeMaker {
   private Shape circle;
   private Shape rectangle;
   private Shape square;

   public ShapeMaker() {
      circle = new Circle();
      rectangle = new Rectangle();
      square = new Square();
   }

   public void drawCircle(){
      circle.draw();
   }

   public void drawRectangle(){
      rectangle.draw();
   }

   public void drawSquare(){
      square.draw();
   }
}

public class FacadePatternDemo {
   public static void main(String[] args) {
      ShapeMaker shapeMaker = new ShapeMaker();
```

```
        shapeMaker.drawCircle();
        shapeMaker.drawRectangle();
        shapeMaker.drawSquare();
    }
}
```

In the above example, we have a ShapeMaker that simplifies the interface to a set of Shape classes. The client code only needs to call methods on the ShapeMaker and doesn't need to know about the individual Shape classes. This simplifies the usage of the Shape classes for the client code.

3.8 Describe how the Command pattern can be combined with the Composite pattern to create complex commands.

The Command pattern is a widely-used design pattern that separates the execution of a command from its invocation. It is particularly useful when we need to encapsulate the request, parameters, and execution details of a particular operation.

The Composite pattern, on the other hand, is a design pattern that allows you to compose objects into tree structures to represent part-whole hierarchies.

When used together, the Command pattern and Composite pattern can create complex commands that can execute a set of sub-commands in a structured manner. This is particularly useful when there is a need to execute a command that involves multiple sub-commands that need to be executed in a particular order, or when we want to treat a group of commands as a single command.

To implement complex commands using the Command and
Composite pattern, we can create a composite command object that uses the Command pattern to define each individual
sub-command. The composite object can then execute the individual commands in a predetermined order.

Let's consider an example to illustrate this concept. Suppose
we have a drawing program that allows users to draw shapes on
a canvas. Each shape is represented as a separate object with
its own set of properties such as size, location, and color. We
want to create a composite command that allows us to draw a
complex shape that is composed of multiple sub-shapes.

First, we would create an interface for the Command pattern
to define the structure of individual commands. In our case,
we can define a 'Drawable' interface with a 'draw' method that
takes a 'Canvas' object as a parameter:

```
public interface Drawable {
    void draw(Canvas canvas);
}
```

Next, we can create implementations of the 'Drawable' interface
for each of the sub-shapes that make up our complex shape.
For example, we can create a 'Rectangle' class that draws a
rectangle on the canvas:

```
public class Rectangle implements Drawable {
    private int x,
    private int y;
    private int width;
    private int height;
    private Color color;

    public Rectangle(int x, int y, int width, int height, Color color
        ) {
        this.x = x;
        this.y = y;
        this.width = width;
        this.height = height;
        this.color = color;
    }
}
```

```
    @Override
    public void draw(Canvas canvas) {
        canvas.drawRect(x, y, width, height, color);
    }
}
```

Similarly, we can create a 'Circle' class that draws a circle on the canvas:

```
public class Circle implements Drawable {
    private int x;
    private int y;
    private int radius;
    private Color color;

    public Circle(int x, int y, int radius, Color color) {
        this.x = x;
        this.y = y;
        this.radius = radius;
        this.color = color;
    }

    @Override
    public void draw(Canvas canvas) {
        canvas.drawCircle(x, y, radius, color);
    }
}
```

Now that we have defined our individual commands, we can use the Composite pattern to define a complex command that is composed of multiple sub-commands. We can create a 'ComplexShape' class that holds a list of 'Drawable' objects and can execute each of them in the order that they were added.

```
public class ComplexShape implements Drawable {
    private List<Drawable> shapes = new ArrayList<>();

    public void addShape(Drawable shape) {
        shapes.add(shape);
    }

    @Override
    public void draw(Canvas canvas) {
        for (Drawable shape : shapes) {
            shape.draw(canvas);
        }
    }
}
```

Finally, we can use our composite 'ComplexShape' command
just like any other 'Drawable' command. For example, we can
create a new 'Canvas' object and add a 'ComplexShape' that is
composed of a 'Rectangle' and a 'Circle':

```
Canvas canvas = new Canvas();
ComplexShape complexShape = new ComplexShape();
complexShape.addShape(new Rectangle(10, 10, 100, 50, Color.RED));
complexShape.addShape(new Circle(50, 50, 25, Color.BLUE));
canvas.draw(complexShape);
```

This code will draw a complex shape that consists of a red
rectangle and a blue circle on the canvas.

In conclusion, the Command and Composite patterns can be
used together to create complex commands that execute a set
of sub-commands in a structured manner. The Command pattern provides a way to encapsulate individual commands, while
the Composite pattern provides a way to compose multiple commands into a single complex command.

3.9   Explain the benefits of using shallow copying and deep copying in the Prototype pattern.

The Prototype pattern is a creational pattern that allows creating new objects by cloning a prototype object instead of creating a new one from scratch. The prototype object serves as
a blueprint for creating new objects with the same properties
and behaviors.

In the Prototype pattern, there are two types of copying: shallow copying and deep copying. Shallow copying creates a new

object but shares its internal state with the original prototype object. Deep copying creates a new object and copies all of the prototype's internal state to the new object.

The benefits of using shallow copying and deep copying in the Prototype pattern are as follows:

1. Shallow Copying
When an object is shallow copied, a new object is created with the same values for each field as the original object. If some fields of the object are references to other objects, then the new object will have references to the same objects as the original object. It means that changes to the referenced objects will affect both the original object and the new object. If the object contains mutable state that is shared among multiple objects, shallow copying helps prevent duplication of the mutable state.

For example, suppose we have a Person class that contains an array of phone numbers that they own. A shallow copy implementation will create a new Person object, but both the original and new Person objects will reference the same phone numbers array. If we update the phone numbers array in the original person object, the changes will be reflected in the new person object as well.

Here is an example of shallow copying in Java using the clone() method:

```
public class Person implements Cloneable {
    private String name;
    private String[] phoneNumbers;

    public Person(String name, String[] phoneNumbers) {
        this.name = name;
        this.phoneNumbers = phoneNumbers;
    }

    public void setPhoneNumbers(String[] phoneNumbers) {
        this.phoneNumbers = phoneNumbers;
```

```
    }
    public Object clone() {
        try {
            return super.clone();
        } catch(CloneNotSupportedException e) {
            return null;
        }
    }
}

//Shallow copy example
String[] phoneNumbers = {"555-1234", "555-5678"};
Person prototype = new Person("John␣Doe", phoneNumbers);

Person clone = (Person) prototype.clone();
System.out.println(clone.getName()); //John Doe
clone.setPhoneNumbers(new String[]{"555-4444", "555-5555"});
System.out.println(prototype.getPhoneNumbers()[0]); //555-4444
```

In this example, when we set the phone numbers of the clone object, the phone numbers of the prototype object are updated as well.

2. Deep Copying

When an object is deep copied, a new object is created with its own copy of all the fields and the objects they reference. It means that changes to the new object's internal state will not affect the original object's state. Deep copying is useful if the original object contains objects with mutable state we want to change independently.

For example, consider the same Person class example as before, but now with a mutable Address object that contains street, city and zipCode fields. If we create a deep copy of the Person object, we want a new Address object to be created as well, giving each Person object its own copy of the mutable Address object.

Here is an example of deep copying in Java using serialization:

```
public class Address implements Serializable {
    private String street;
    private String city;
    private String zipCode;

    //getters and setters
}

public class Person implements Serializable {
    private String name;
    private Address address;

    public Person(String name, Address address) {
        this.name = name;
        this.address = address;
    }

    // Getters and setters

    public Person deepCopy() throws IOException,
        ClassNotFoundException {
        ByteArrayOutputStream byteArrayOutputStream = new
            ByteArrayOutputStream();
        ObjectOutputStream objectOutputStream = new
            ObjectOutputStream(byteArrayOutputStream);
        objectOutputStream.writeObject(this);

        ByteArrayInputStream byteArrayInputStream =
            new ByteArrayInputStream(byteArrayOutputStream.
                toByteArray());
        ObjectInputStream objectInputStream = new ObjectInputStream(
            byteArrayInputStream);
        return (Person) objectInputStream.readObject();
    }
}

//Deep copy example
Address address = new Address("123 Main St", "Anytown", "12345");
Person prototype = new Person("John Doe", address);

Person clone = prototype.deepCopy();
address.setZipCode("67890");

System.out.println(clone.getAddress().getZipCode()); //12345
System.out.println(prototype.getAddress().getZipCode()); //67890
```

In this example, when we set the zip code property of the address object in the original person object, it does not affect the zip code of the clone person object because we created a new address object in the deep copy process.

To sum up, the Prototype pattern provides great benefits for object creation by allowing objects to be created from a prototype object. Using shallow and deep copying can further enhance the pattern's benefits, depending on the application's requirements. Shallow copying is useful to prevent duplication of the mutable state of an object, whereas deep copying creates independent copies of an object's mutable state.

3.10   Can you discuss the advantages and disadvantages of using the Builder pattern with a Fluent Interface?

The Builder pattern is a creational design pattern that separates the construction of complex objects from their representation. The pattern uses a separate builder object that receives instructions on how to construct an object. The Fluent Interface is a design pattern that allows us to write code that is easy to read and understand by chaining methods together in a fluent manner. In this pattern, each method on the fluent interface returns the modified object. By combining the Builder pattern with a Fluent Interface, we can create an API that is more readable, expressive, and flexible.

Advantages:
1. Readability: Fluent Interface makes the API more readable and understandable by providing method chaining. This means that it is easier to understand what is happening and what the code does.

2. Expressiveness: Using a Fluent Interface, we can express very complex operations in a readable and concise manner.

Complex operations can be broken down into smaller, more manageable parts, which are easier to understand and maintain.

3. Flexibility: The use of the Builder pattern with a Fluent Interface allows us to change the order of operations, add or remove steps or customize the construction process easily. This increases the flexibility of our API.

4. Validation: The Builder pattern enables us to validate the inputs for the construction process, providing more control over error conditions.

Disadvantages:
1. Overhead: The use of the Builder pattern for simple objects can create unnecessary overhead. A simple constructor may be more efficient.

2. Complexity: Combining the Builder pattern with a Fluent Interface can sometimes result in complex and hard-to-understand code, especially when dealing with many different options and settings.

3. Learning curve: While using a Fluent Interface is generally easy to understand, combining it with the Builder pattern can create a steep learning curve for new developers.

Here is an example of using the Builder pattern with a Fluent Interface in Java:

```
public class Product {
    private String name;
    private String description;
    private double price;

    public static class Builder {
        private String name;
        private String description;
        private double price;
```

```
public Builder setName(String name) {
    this.name = name;
    return this;
}

public Builder setDescription(String description) {
    this.description = description;
    return this;
}

public Builder setPrice(double price) {
    this.price = price;
    return this;
}

public Product build() {
    return new Product(this);
}
    }

    private Product(Builder builder) {
        this.name = builder.name;
        this.description = builder.description;
        this.price = builder.price;
    }

    // Getters
}

// Usage
Product product = new Product.Builder()
        .setName("Phone")
        .setDescription("This is a phone")
        .setPrice(800.0)
        .build();
```

In this example, we used the Builder pattern to create a 'Product' object with three properties: 'name', 'description' and 'price'. We then used a fluent interface to set the values of these properties. The 'build' method returns the constructed 'Product' object. Overall, the use of the fluent interface makes it easy to understand and creates an expressive API that can be easily modified.

3.11 How can the Facade pattern be used in a microservices architecture to simplify communication between services?

Microservices architecture emphasizes the creation of small, autonomous services that work together to deliver a complete application. Each microservice has its own logic and functionality and communicates with other microservices via APIs. However, as the number of microservices grows, the complexity of communication between them can increase, leading to integration issues and dependencies. This is where the Facade pattern can be useful.

The Facade pattern is a structural pattern that provides a simplified interface to a complex system. It encapsulates the complexity of the system and provides a unified interface that can be used by clients. In a microservices architecture, a Facade can be used to provide a simplified interface for communication between services.

The Facade can provide a single API that abstracts away the details of communicating with multiple microservices. This simplifies the client's interaction with the system and can improve the overall performance of the system by reducing the number of requests made by the client.

Let's consider an example. Suppose we have a microservices architecture for an e-commerce application. The microservices include:

 - Product service: responsible for managing product information
 - Order service: responsible for managing orders

- Payment service: responsible for processing payments

Suppose a client wants to place an order. The client needs to interact with all three microservices to complete the order. The client needs to:

- Get product information from the Product service
- Create an order using the Order service
- Process payment using the Payment service

Without a Facade, the client needs to make separate requests to each microservice. This can lead to slow performance and higher latency. With the Facade pattern, we can create a single API that abstracts away the details of communicating with multiple microservices.

For example, we can create an OrderFacade that provides a simplified interface for placing an order. The OrderFacade internally interacts with the Product service, Order service, and Payment service to complete the order. The client only needs to interact with the OrderFacade and does not need to be aware of the details of how the order is processed.

Here's an example in Java:

```java
public class OrderFacade {
    private ProductService productService;
    private OrderService orderService;
    private PaymentService paymentService;

    public OrderFacade(ProductService productService, OrderService
        orderService, PaymentService paymentService) {
        this.productService = productService;
        this.orderService = orderService;
        this.paymentService = paymentService;
    }

    public void placeOrder(Order order) {
        // Get product information
        Product product = productService.getProduct(order.getProductId()
```

```
        );

    // Create order
    orderService.createOrder(order);

    // Process payment
    paymentService.processPayment(order.getTotalAmount());
  }
}
```

In this example, the OrderFacade provides a 'placeOrder' method that internally calls the 'getProduct' method on the Product-Service, the 'createOrder' method on the OrderService, and the 'processPayment' method on the PaymentService. The client only needs to interact with the OrderFacade and does not need to call each microservice separately.

In summary, the Facade pattern can be used in a microservices architecture to simplify communication between services, abstract away the details of communicating with multiple microservices, and improve the overall performance of the system.

3.12 Explain how the Chain of Responsibility pattern can be used to implement a centralized error handling mechanism.

The Chain of Responsibility pattern allows multiple objects to handle a request without knowing which object will handle it. This pattern can be used to implement a centralized error handling mechanism.

In this context, the Chain of Responsibility pattern would work as follows: each layer of the system (such as the data access

layer, the business logic layer, or the presentation layer) would
have its own error handler. These error handlers would be ar-
ranged in a chain of responsibility, where each error handler
would be responsible for handling a specific type of error.

When an error occurs in the system, it would be caught by the
first error handler in the chain. If that error handler cannot
handle the error, it would pass the error on to the next error
handler in the chain, and so on, until the error is either handled
or there are no more error handlers to pass it to.

This approach has several advantages. First, it keeps error handling code organized and modular, allowing different parts of
the system to have their own specific error handling logic. Second, it provides a centralized error handling mechanism, ensuring that all errors in the system are handled consistently.
Third, it allows new error handlers to be easily added to the
system as new types of errors are encountered or as existing
error handling code is refactored.

Here is an example Java implementation of the Chain of Responsibility pattern for error handling:

```java
public abstract class ErrorHandler {
    private ErrorHandler nextHandler;

    public void setNextHandler(ErrorHandler handler) {
        this.nextHandler = handler;
    }

    public void handleError(Error error) {
        if (canHandle(error)) {
            handle(error);
        } else if (nextHandler != null) {
            nextHandler.handleError(error);
        } else {
            // no error handler was able to handle this error
            throw new RuntimeException("Unhandled error: " + error.
                getMessage());
        }
    }
}
```

```
    protected abstract boolean canHandle(Error error);

    protected abstract void handle(Error error);
}

public class DataAccessErrorHandler extends ErrorHandler {
    @Override
    protected boolean canHandle(Error error) {
        // check if this error is a data access error
        return error instanceof DataAccessError;
    }

    @Override
    protected void handle(Error error) {
        // handle the data access error
        // ...
    }
}

public class BusinessLogicErrorHandler extends ErrorHandler {
    @Override
    protected boolean canHandle(Error error) {
        // check if this error is a business logic error
        return error instanceof BusinessLogicError;
    }

    @Override
    protected void handle(Error error) {
        // handle the business logic error
        // ...
    }
}

public class PresentationErrorHandler extends ErrorHandler {
    @Override
    protected boolean canHandle(Error error) {
        // check if this error is a presentation error
        return error instanceof PresentationError;
    }

    @Override
    protected void handle(Error error) {
        // handle the presentation error
        // ...
    }
}
```

In this example, the 'ErrorHandler' class is the abstract base class for all error handlers. Each concrete error handler (such as 'DataAccessErrorHandler', 'BusinessLogicErrorHandler', and 'Pre-

sentationErrorHandler') extends 'ErrorHandler' and overrides
the 'canHandle' and 'handle' methods.

The 'canHandle' method checks if the error that was passed to
the error handler can be handled by that error handler. If it
can, the 'handle' method is called to actually handle the error.
If not, the error is passed on to the next error handler in the
chain by calling 'nextHandler.handleError(error)'.

To use this error handling mechanism in our system, we would
create an instance of each of the concrete error handlers and
link them together in a chain of responsibility:

```
public class ErrorHandlerChain {
    private ErrorHandler firstHandler;

    public ErrorHandlerChain() {
        DataAccessErrorHandler dataAccessHandler = new
            DataAccessErrorHandler();
        BusinessLogicErrorHandler businessLogicHandler = new
            BusinessLogicErrorHandler();
        PresentationErrorHandler presentationHandler = new
            PresentationErrorHandler();

        dataAccessHandler.setNextHandler(businessLogicHandler);
        businessLogicHandler.setNextHandler(presentationHandler);

        firstHandler = dataAccessHandler;
    }

    public void handleError(Error error) {
        firstHandler.handleError(error);
    }
}
```

In this example, the 'ErrorHandlerChain' class creates the instance of each concrete error handler and sets their next handlers. The 'handleError' method in the 'ErrorHandlerChain'
class is the entry point for error handling in the system. When
an error occurs, we would call 'handleError' with the error object. The error would then be passed down the chain of responsibility until it is handled or until there are no more error

handlers to pass it to.

3.13 Can you provide an example of using the Iterator pattern with the Composite pattern to traverse a complex structure?

The Iterator pattern provides a way to access elements of an aggregate object sequentially without exposing its underlying representation. The Composite pattern allows us to treat a group of objects in the same way as a single object. In this answer, we will combine these two patterns to traverse a complex hierarchical structure composed of multiple components.

Let's consider a file system as an example of a complex structure. The file system can contain directories, which can contain files and subdirectories, and so on. We can represent this structure using the Composite pattern, where each component can be a file or a directory, and a directory can contain other directories and files.

To make it easy to traverse the file system, we will use the Iterator pattern to provide a way to access the elements of the composite structure. We can define an interface 'Iterator' to represent the iterator, and a concrete class 'FileSystemIterator' to implement it.

```
interface Iterator<T> {
    public boolean hasNext();
    public T next();
}

class FileSystemIterator implements Iterator<Component> {
    // Implementation of the Iterator interface
```

```
    // Traverse the composite structure and return the components one
        by one
}
```

Next, we can define the 'Component' interface and its concrete classes 'File' and 'Directory' to represent the elements of the composite structure.

```
interface Component {
    public void add(Component component);
    public void remove(Component component);
    public Iterator<Component> iterator();
}

class File implements Component {
    // Implementation of the Component interface for files
}

class Directory implements Component {
    private List<Component> components = new ArrayList<Component>();
    // Implementation of the Component interface for directories
    // Add and remove components from the list
    // Return a FileSystemIterator to traverse the directory
        components
}
```

In the 'Directory' class, we have a list to store the components of the directory, and we implement the 'add', 'remove', and 'iterator' methods of the 'Component' interface. The 'add' and 'remove' methods can be used to modify the list, while the 'iterator' method returns an instance of the 'FileSystemIterator' to traverse the children of the directory.

Finally, we can use the 'FileSystemIterator' to traverse the file system in a depth-first manner. Here is an example code snippet:

```
Component root = /* initialize the root directory */;
Iterator<Component> iterator = new FileSystemIterator(root);
while (iterator.hasNext()) {
    Component component = iterator.next();
    // Do something with the component, e.g. print its name
}
```

In this code, we initialize the 'root' directory and create a 'FileSystemIterator' to traverse its components. We then use a while loop and the 'next' method of the iterator to access the components one by one, and perform some action on each component, such as printing its name.

In conclusion, the Iterator pattern can be combined with the Composite pattern to traverse complex hierarchical structures, such as file systems. The Iterator provides a way to access the elements of the composite structure in a sequential manner, while the Composite allows us to treat the group of objects in the same way as a single object. The resulting implementation is flexible, extensible, and easy to use.

3.14 How does the Flyweight pattern interact with the Garbage Collection mechanism in languages like Java and C#?

The Flyweight pattern is a software design pattern that aims to minimize memory usage by sharing as much data as possible among similar objects. This is achieved by separating the intrinsic (shared) state and extrinsic (non-shared) state of objects, and storing the intrinsic state in a Flyweight Factory that can be shared by multiple objects.

The Garbage Collection mechanism in languages like Java and C# is responsible for reclaiming the memory used by objects that are no longer referenced by any other object in the program. This mechanism periodically runs in the background, automatically freeing up memory that is no longer in use.

The Flyweight pattern interacts with the Garbage Collection mechanism in two ways:

1. Shared Flyweight objects are not eligible for Garbage Collection until all objects that reference them are also eligible for Garbage Collection. This is because these objects are still being used by other objects and should not be deleted prematurely.

2. Flyweight Factories themselves can be eligible for Garbage Collection if there are no objects that reference them. This can happen if all objects that use the Flyweight Factory to create Flyweight objects are themselves no longer referenced by any other object in the program.

Here's an example of how shared Flyweight objects are handled by the Garbage Collection mechanism in Java:

```java
// Flyweight Factory class
class FlyweightFactory {
    private static Map<String, Flyweight> flyweights = new HashMap
        <>();

    // Flyweight creation method
    public static Flyweight getFlyweight(String intrinsicState) {
        if (!flyweights.containsKey(intrinsicState)) {
            flyweights.put(intrinsicState, new ConcreteFlyweight(
                intrinsicState));
        }
        return flyweights.get(intrinsicState);
    }
}

// Flyweight interface
interface Flyweight {
    void operation(String extrinsicState);
}

// Concrete Flyweight class
class ConcreteFlyweight implements Flyweight {
    private String intrinsicState;

    public ConcreteFlyweight(String intrinsicState) {
        this.intrinsicState = intrinsicState;
    }
```

```
    @Override
    public void operation(String extrinsicState) {
        System.out.println("Intrinsic state: " + this.intrinsicState)
            ;
        System.out.println("Extrinsic state: " + extrinsicState);
    }
}

// Client class
class Client {
    public static void main(String[] args) {
        Flyweight flyweight1 = FlyweightFactory.getFlyweight("a");
        Flyweight flyweight2 = FlyweightFactory.getFlyweight("a");
        Flyweight flyweight3 = FlyweightFactory.getFlyweight("b");

        flyweight1.operation("1");
        flyweight2.operation("2");
        flyweight3.operation("3");

        flyweight1 = null; // set reference to null
        flyweight2 = null; // set reference to null

        // Garbage Collection may not happen immediately, but once it
            does, the shared
        // Flyweight object with intrinsic state "a" will not be
            deleted until flyweight3
        // is also eligible for Garbage Collection
    }
}
```

In this example, the Flyweight Factory is implemented as a Singleton that stores all shared Flyweight objects in a HashMap. The 'getFlyweight' method first checks if a Flyweight object with the given intrinsic state already exists in the map, and if not, creates a new one and adds it to the map. This ensures that only one shared Flyweight object with a given intrinsic state exists in the program.

The 'operation' method of the Concrete Flyweight class takes an extrinsic state as a parameter, but only uses it for outputting information to the console. The intrinsic state is always the same for all shared Flyweight objects with the same intrinsic state.

In the Client class, three Flyweight objects are created using the
Flyweight Factory. The first two have the same intrinsic state
("a"), and so are both references to the same shared object.
The third object has a different intrinsic state ("b"), so a new
Flyweight object is created for it.

After the Flyweight objects are used to do some work, their
references are set to null, indicating that they are no longer
needed. The Garbage Collection mechanism may not immediately delete the shared Flyweight object with intrinsic state "a",
since it is still being used by the third object. However, once
that object is also no longer referenced by any other object in
the program, the shared Flyweight object can be safely deleted.

3.15   Explain the role of the Mediator pattern in reducing coupling between components in a GUI framework.

The Mediator pattern is a behavioral design pattern that allows
for the communication between a set of objects to be mediated
by a single object, called the Mediator. This pattern is suitable
when a system involves many objects that interact in complex
ways, creating unwanted dependencies between them. By introducing a Mediator object to handle this communication, we
can reduce the coupling between components and improve the
maintainability and modifiability of the system.

In a GUI framework, there are often many different components
that need to communicate with each other. For example, consider a simple window with a button and a text area. When
the button is pressed, the text area should display a message.

Without a Mediator object, the button would need to directly manipulate the text area. This can lead to a tight coupling between the button and the text area, making the system hard to modify and maintain.

Using the Mediator pattern, we can introduce a mediator object that handles the communication between the button and the text area. The button would send a message to the mediator indicating that it was pressed, and the mediator would then update the text area with the appropriate message. This approach decouples the button from the text area, allowing them to be modified independently of each other.

Here is an example of how the Mediator pattern could be used in a GUI framework, using Java code. We will create a simple window with a button and a text area, and use a Mediator object to handle the communication between them:

```java
// Define the Mediator interface
interface Mediator {
    void buttonPressed();
}

// Define the Button class
class Button {
    private Mediator mediator;

    public Button(Mediator mediator) {
        this.mediator = mediator;
    }

    public void press() {
        mediator.buttonPressed();
    }
}

// Define the TextArea class
class TextArea {
    public void displayMessage(String message) {
        System.out.println(message);
    }
}

// Define the Window class that uses the Mediator pattern
```

```
class Window implements Mediator {
    private Button button;
    private TextArea textArea;

    public Window() {
        textArea = new TextArea();
        button = new Button(this);
    }

    public void buttonPressed() {
        textArea.displayMessage("Button was pressed");
    }

    public void show() {
        // Code to display the window
        button.press();
    }
}

// Usage example
Window window = new Window();
window.show();
```

In this example, we have defined a Mediator interface that defines the method for handling button presses. The Button class takes in a Mediator object during construction and calls the 'buttonPressed()' method on it when the button is pressed. The TextArea class simply displays messages.

The Window class acts as the Mediator object, implementing the Mediator interface. When the Window is created, it creates the Button and TextArea objects, passing in 'this' as the Mediator. When the button is pressed, the 'buttonPressed()' method is called on the Window, which in turn updates the TextArea with the appropriate message.

By using a Mediator object to handle the communication between the button and the text area, we have reduced the coupling between these components, making the system easier to modify and maintain.

3.16   How does the Proxy pattern differ from the Adapter pattern in terms of intent and implementation?

Both the Proxy pattern and the Adapter pattern are part of the structural design patterns category, and while they might look similar at the first glance, they have different intents and implementations.

Proxy Pattern:
The Proxy pattern aims to provide a substitute or placeholder for another object to control access to it. In simple words, we can say that a proxy is a stand-in or placeholder for another object. It provides the same interface as the real object, so we can interchange them without changing the code that uses them. The proxy class acts as an intermediary between the client and the target object, hiding any implementation details of the target object from the client.

Implementation of Proxy Pattern:

The Proxy pattern follows the same interface as the target object, and also holds a reference to a target object. The Proxy object, before forwarding calls to target object, can add its functionality like caching, logging, or controlling the access to target object. This shielding of target object provides a level of security since the client can't access the target object directly. The following is a simple implementation of the proxy pattern:

```
// Subject Interface
public interface Image {
    void display();
}

// Real Object implements the subject interface
```

```java
public class RealImage implements Image {
    private String filename;

    public RealImage(String filename) {
        this.filename = filename;
        loadImageFromDisk();
    }

    private void loadImageFromDisk() {
        System.out.println("Loading " + filename);
    }

    public void display() {
        System.out.println("Displaying " + filename);
    }
}

// Proxy class implements the subject interface
public class ProxyImage implements Image {
    private Image realImage;
    private String filename;

    public ProxyImage(String filename) {
        this.filename = filename;
    }

    public void display() {
        if (realImage == null) {
            realImage = new RealImage(filename);
        }
        realImage.display();
    }
}
```

Adapter Pattern:

The Adapter pattern aims to convert one interface into another interface, so that two different incompatible classes can interact with each other. To put it simply, an adapter class is like a language translator, allowing two incompatible interfaces to communicate with each other.

Implementation of Adapter Pattern:

The Adapter pattern implements the Target interface and instantiates an adapter object that wraps an Adaptee object, which implements the Adaptee interface. The Target interface specifies the client's requirements while the Adapter interface implements the Adaptee interface for satisfying the client request. An example implementation of the Adapter pattern is given below:

```
//Target Interface
interface AdvancedMediaPlayer {
   void playVlc(String fileName);
   void playMp4(String fileName);
}

//Adaptee classes
class VlcPlayer implements AdvancedMediaPlayer {
   public void playVlc(String fileName) {
       System.out.println("Playing vlc file. Name: "+ fileName);
   }

   public void playMp4(String fileName) {
     //do nothing
   }
}

class Mp4Player implements AdvancedMediaPlayer{

   public void playVlc(String fileName) {
     //do nothing
   }

   public void playMp4(String fileName) {
       System.out.println("Playing mp4 file. Name: "+ fileName);
   }
}

//Adapter class
class MediaAdapter implements MediaPlayer {

   AdvancedMediaPlayer advancedMusicPlayer;

    public MediaAdapter(String audioType){
      if(audioType.equalsIgnoreCase("vlc") ){
        advancedMusicPlayer = new VlcPlayer();

      }else if (audioType.equalsIgnoreCase("mp4")){
        advancedMusicPlayer = new Mp4Player();
      }
   }

   public void play(String audioType, String fileName) {

      if(audioType.equalsIgnoreCase("vlc")){
```

```
        advancedMusicPlayer.playVlc(fileName);
    }
    else if(audioType.equalsIgnoreCase("mp4")){
        advancedMusicPlayer.playMp4(fileName);
    }   /
  }
}

//Target class
class AudioPlayer implements MediaPlayer {
  MediaAdapter mediaAdapter;

  public void play(String audioType, String fileName) {

    //inbuilt support to play mp3 music files
    if(audioType.equalsIgnoreCase("mp3")){
      System.out.println("Playing mp3 file. Name: "+ fileName);
    }

    //mediaAdapter is providing support to play other file formats
    else if(audioType.equalsIgnoreCase("vlc") || audioType.
        equalsIgnoreCase("mp4")){
      mediaAdapter = new MediaAdapter(audioType);
      mediaAdapter.play(audioType, fileName);
    }

    else{
      System.out.println("Invalid media. " + audioType + " format
          not supported");
    }
  }
}
```

Key Differences:

* The Proxy pattern acts as a placeholder or stand-in for an object, while the Adapter pattern acts as a wrapper for an object.

* The Adapter pattern is used to convert one interface into another, while the Proxy pattern is used to implement control behavior of the target object through the proxy object.

* Proxy pattern shields target object from direct access by the client, while the adapter pattern does not necessarily do that.

* In Proxy pattern, the proxy object has the same interface as the target object, while in adapter pattern, the adapter object is wrapped around adaptee object with a different interface that sat-

isfies the client's requirement.

To sum up, the Proxy pattern is used as a placeholder or a wrapper for another object, while the Adapter pattern is used as a bridge between two incompatible interfaces.

3.17   Describe a scenario where using the Bridge pattern would be more advantageous than using multiple inheritance.

The Bridge pattern is a structural design pattern that decouples an abstraction from its implementation, allowing them to vary independently. On the other hand, multiple inheritance allows a class to inherit from multiple parent classes, where the child class inherits the behavior and characteristics of all parent classes.

There are certain scenarios where using the Bridge pattern would be more advantageous than using multiple inheritance. One such scenario is when we have a hierarchy of abstractions and multiple implementations, and we want to be able to vary them independently.

Suppose, we have a drawing application that can draw different shapes like Circle, Rectangle, Triangle, etc. The application supports two types of rendering - on screen and in a file. We could have a hierarchy of shapes and a hierarchy of renderers, resulting in 4 possible shape/renderer combinations.

With the Bridge pattern, we can create an abstraction for the shape hierarchy and another abstraction for the renderer hierarchy, and then bridge them. The bridge interface will then be responsible for drawing the shape in the specified renderer. The advantage of this approach is that we can add new shapes and renderers without affecting existing code.

On the other hand, if we were to use multiple inheritance, we would have to create multiple classes for each shape/renderer combination, resulting in a lot of duplication of code. This approach becomes unmanageable for larger hierarchies and combinations.

Here is an example demonstrating the use of the Bridge pattern in a drawing application:

```java
// Abstraction for shape
abstract class Shape {
   protected Renderer renderer;

   public Shape(Renderer renderer) {
      this.renderer = renderer;
   }

   public abstract void draw();
}

// Concrete implementation of shape
class Circle extends Shape {
   public Circle(Renderer renderer) {
      super(renderer);
   }
   @Override
   public void draw() {
      renderer.renderCircle();
   }
}

// Abstraction for renderer
interface Renderer {
   void renderCircle();
   void renderRectangle();
   void renderTriangle();
}

// Concrete implementation of renderer for screen
```

```
class ScreenRenderer implements Renderer {
  @Override
  public void renderCircle() {
    // code to render circle on screen
  }

  @Override
  public void renderRectangle() {
    // code to render rectangle on screen
  }

  @Override
  public void renderTriangle() {
    // code to render triangle on screen
  }
}

// Concrete implementation of renderer for file
class FileRenderer implements Renderer {
  @Override
  public void renderCircle() {
    // code to render circle in file
  }

  @Override
  public void renderRectangle() {
    // code to render rectangle in file
  }

  @Override
  public void renderTriangle() {
    // code to render triangle in file
  }
}

// Client code
public class DrawingClient {
  public static void main(String[] args) {
    Renderer screenRenderer = new ScreenRenderer();
    Renderer fileRenderer = new FileRenderer();

    Shape circle = new Circle(screenRenderer);
    Shape rectangle = new Rectangle(fileRenderer);

    circle.draw();
    rectangle.draw();
  }
}
```

In the above example, the Shape abstraction is bridged with the
Renderer interface to draw the shapes in different renderers, i.e.,
screen and file. This approach is more flexible and scalable, as

we can add new shapes and renderers without affecting existing code.

3.18   Can you provide an example of combining the Template Method pattern with the Factory Method pattern for extensibility and flexibility?

We can combine the Template Method and Factory Method design patterns to achieve flexibility and extensibility in our code. The Template Method pattern is used when we want to define the skeleton of an algorithm in base class while allowing derived classes to override some specific steps of the algorithm. The Factory Method pattern is used when we want to delegate the responsibility of creating objects to the derived classes, allowing us to create objects of different types at runtime.

Let's say we are building a framework to process different types of documents (e.g., PDF, Word, Excel, etc.). We want to define a base class for all types of documents, while allowing derived classes to override specific steps of the document processing algorithm. Additionally, we want to be able to create different types of documents at runtime, so we will use the Factory Method pattern.

Here's an example implementation:

```
public abstract class DocumentProcessor {

    // Template Method pattern
    public final void processDocument() {
        openDocument();
        readDocument();
        parseDocument();
```

```
        // Hook method
        if (shouldCompressDocument()) {
            compressDocument();
        }
        writeDocument();
        closeDocument();
    }

    private void openDocument() {
        // Default implementation
    }

    protected abstract void readDocument();

    protected abstract void parseDocument();

    // Hook method
    protected boolean shouldCompressDocument() {
        return false; // Default implementation
    }

    private void compressDocument() {
        // Default implementation
    }

    protected abstract void writeDocument();

    private void closeDocument() {
        // Default implementation
    }

    // Factory Method pattern
    public static DocumentProcessor createDocumentProcessor(String
        documentType) {
        switch (documentType) {
            case "PDF":
                return new PdfDocumentProcessor();
            case "Word":
                return new WordDocumentProcessor();
            case "Excel":
                return new ExcelDocumentProcessor();
            // Add cases for other document types here
            default:
                throw new IllegalArgumentException("Invalid␣document␣
                    type:␣" + documentType);
        }
    }
}

public class PdfDocumentProcessor extends DocumentProcessor {
    protected void readDocument() {
        // Implementation for reading a PDF document
    }
```

```
    protected void parseDocument() {
        // Implementation for parsing a PDF document
    }

    protected void writeDocument() {
        // Implementation for writing a PDF document
    }
}

public class WordDocumentProcessor extends DocumentProcessor {
    protected void readDocument() {
        // Implementation for reading a Word document
    }

    protected void parseDocument() {
        // Implementation for parsing a Word document
    }

    protected void writeDocument() {
        // Implementation for writing a Word document
    }
}

public class ExcelDocumentProcessor extends DocumentProcessor {
    protected void readDocument() {
        // Implementation for reading an Excel document
    }

    protected void parseDocument() {
        // Implementation for parsing an Excel document
    }

    protected void writeDocument() {
        // Implementation for writing an Excel document
    }

    // Override Hook method
    protected boolean shouldCompressDocument() {
        return true;
    }
}
```

In this example, we have defined a 'DocumentProcessor' base
class that implements the document processing algorithm using the Template Method pattern. The 'openDocument()',
'compressDocument()', and 'closeDocument()' methods have
default implementations, while the 'readDocument()', 'parse-
Document()', and 'writeDocument()' methods are abstract and
must be implemented by derived classes.

We have also defined a 'shouldCompressDocument()' hook method that can be optionally overridden by derived classes to modify the behavior of the algorithm. In the 'ExcelDocumentProcessor' class, we have overridden this hook method to enable document compression.

Finally, we have created a 'createDocumentProcessor()' factory method in the 'DocumentProcessor' class that returns an instance of a specific document processor based on the provided document type. This method can be extended to add support for additional document types.

Using this implementation, we can create different types of document processors at runtime:

```
DocumentProcessor pdfProcessor = DocumentProcessor.
    createDocumentProcessor("PDF");
pdfProcessor.processDocument();

DocumentProcessor wordProcessor = DocumentProcessor.
    createDocumentProcessor("Word");
wordProcessor.processDocument();

DocumentProcessor excelProcessor = DocumentProcessor.
    createDocumentProcessor("Excel");
excelProcessor.processDocument();
```

This provides us with the flexibility and extensibility we need, as we can add new document types and override specific steps of the document processing algorithm as needed.

3.19 Discuss the trade-offs between using the Abstract Factory pattern and the Prototype pattern for object creation.

Both Abstract Factory and Prototype patterns provide solutions for object creation but differ in their implementation and the trade-offs associated with each approach.

Abstract Factory pattern is a creational pattern that provides an interface for creating families of related objects without specifying their concrete classes. It defines an abstract class or interface for creating families of objects, where each family of objects is created by a corresponding concrete factory. The abstract factory is responsible for creating objects of its own family, and these objects typically share a common theme or purpose.

A concrete implementation of the abstract factory offers specific implementations of the factory method which creates these objects. These concrete factories are responsible for creating concrete classes of objects, but the client code does not need to know which concrete implementation will be used.

On the other hand, Prototype pattern is a creational design pattern that allows objects to be created by cloning an existing object. It specifies the kinds of objects to create using a prototypical instance and creates new objects by copying the prototype. This pattern is useful when creating objects is expensive or complicated, and it is more efficient to clone an existing object.

A client creates a new object by asking the prototype object to clone itself. The prototype object can be a concrete implementation, and the client can clone as many instances as needed. Modifications to the clone do not affect the original prototype object, and each clone can be customized to match specific requirements.

Now, let us look at the trade-offs associated with each approach:

1. Flexibility and Configurability:

Abstract Factory pattern offers the flexibility of creating families of related objects, but it is less configurable than the Prototype pattern. The set of objects to be produced is fixed by the concrete implementation of the abstract factory class or interface, whereas in the Prototype pattern, the client can create as many copies of the prototype object as needed and customize each copy differently.

2. Complexity:

Abstract Factory pattern is more complex than the Prototype pattern. It involves creating abstract classes or interfaces, concrete factories for each family of objects, and individual classes for each object in the family. In contrast, the Prototype pattern involves only a prototype object that is cloned to create new instances.

3. Efficiency:

The Prototype pattern is more efficient than the Abstract Factory pattern when creating new objects is expensive or complicated. Cloning an existing object is faster and more efficient than creating a new object from scratch. However, in cases where creating new objects is simple and less expensive, the

Abstract Factory pattern may be preferred.

4. Design Goals:

The choice between the Abstract Factory and Prototype pattern depends on the design goals. If the goal is to create families of related objects, the Abstract Factory pattern is the preferred approach. If the goal is to create copies of existing objects with customization options, the Prototype pattern is more suitable.

In conclusion, both the Abstract Factory and Prototype pattern offer solutions for creating objects, but they differ in their implementation and the trade-offs associated with each approach. The choice between the two patterns depends on the design goals, flexibility, configurability, complexity, and efficiency requirements of the system being designed.

3.20 How can the Visitor pattern be used to perform type-specific operations on a heterogeneous object structure without violating the Liskov Substitution Principle?

The Visitor pattern is used to separate the algorithm logic from the object structure on which it operates, allowing the addition of new operations without having to modify the objects themselves. This pattern can be especially useful when dealing with a heterogeneous object structure, where the type of the object is not known at compile time.

To perform type-specific operations on a heterogeneous object structure without violating the Liskov Substitution Principle, we can use the Visitor pattern in combination with inheritance and polymorphism.

The basic idea of the Visitor pattern is to define a set of "visitors" that can visit each type of object in the structure and perform an operation on them. Each visitor is responsible for implementing the operation for a specific type of object, and can be added or removed without affecting the structure of the objects themselves. The object structure itself does not need to know about the visitors or the operations they perform.

To ensure that the Visitor pattern does not violate the Liskov Substitution Principle, we can use inheritance and polymorphism to ensure that the visitors can handle all types of objects in the structure without knowing their exact type.

Here's an example to demonstrate how the Visitor pattern can be used to perform type-specific operations on a heterogeneous object structure without violating the Liskov Substitution Principle:

```
// Define the object structure
interface Element {
    void accept(Visitor visitor);
}

class ConcreteElementA implements Element {
    void accept(Visitor visitor) {
        visitor.visitElementA(this);
    }

    // methods specific to ConcreteElementA
}

class ConcreteElementB implements Element {
    void accept(Visitor visitor) {
        visitor.visitElementB(this);
    }

    // methods specific to ConcreteElementB
}
```

```
// Define the Visitor interface
interface Visitor {
    void visitElementA(ConcreteElementA element);
    void visitElementB(ConcreteElementB element);
}
// Define the ConcreteVisitor classes
class ConcreteVisitorA implements Visitor {
    void visitElementA(ConcreteElementA element) {
        // perform operation for ConcreteElementA
    }

    void visitElementB(ConcreteElementB element) {
        // perform operation for ConcreteElementB
    }
}

class ConcreteVisitorB implements Visitor {
    void visitElementA(ConcreteElementA element) {
        // perform a different operation for ConcreteElementA
    }

    void visitElementB(ConcreteElementB element) {
        // perform a different operation for ConcreteElementB
    }
}
// Use the Visitor pattern
Element[] elements = { new ConcreteElementA(), new ConcreteElementB
    () };
Visitor visitor = new ConcreteVisitorA();

for (Element element : elements) {
    element.accept(visitor);
}
```

In this example, we define an object structure that consists of two types of elements: ConcreteElementA and ConcreteElementB. We also define a Visitor interface that contains methods for visiting each type of element.

Next, we create two ConcreteVisitor classes that implement the Visitor interface and define the operations to be performed on each type of element.

To iterate over the elements in the object structure, we use a loop and call the accept() method on each element with a Visitor object passed as an argument. This causes the appropriate visit() method to be called on the Visitor object and perform the operation on the element.

By using inheritance and polymorphism, we can ensure that the ConcreteVisitor classes can handle all types of elements without knowing their exact type. This ensures that the Visitor pattern does not violate the Liskov Substitution Principle.

Chapter 4

Advanced

4.1 How can you implement the Singleton pattern in a distributed system to ensure a single instance across multiple servers?

Singleton pattern ensures that only one instance of a class is created and provides a global point of access to that instance. In a distributed system, it is important to ensure that the Singleton instance is available across all servers. This can be achieved by using a centralized mechanism for creating, storing, and accessing the Singleton instance.

One way to implement the Singleton pattern in a distributed system is to use a distributed cache, such as Apache Ignite or Hazelcast. These caching solutions provide the ability to store and access data across multiple servers in a distributed system.

We can use the distributed cache to store the Singleton instance
and ensure that it is available across all servers.

Here's an example implementation of the Singleton pattern using Apache Ignite as the distributed cache:

```java
import org.apache.ignite.Ignite;
import org.apache.ignite.IgniteCache;
import org.apache.ignite.Ignition;

public class Singleton {

    private static final String CACHE_NAME = "singletonCache";
    private static Singleton instance;
    private IgniteCache<String, Singleton> cache;

    private Singleton() {}

    public static synchronized Singleton getInstance() {
        if (instance == null) {
            instance = getInstanceFromCache();
            if (instance == null) {
                instance = new Singleton();
                instance.initialize();
                instance.saveToCache();
            }
        }
        return instance;
    }

    private static Singleton getInstanceFromCache() {
        Ignite ignite = Ignition.start();
        IgniteCache<String, Singleton> cache = ignite.
            getOrCreateCache(CACHE_NAME);
        return cache.get("singletonInstance");
    }

    private void initialize() {
        //initialize the Singleton object
    }

    private void saveToCache() {
        cache.put("singletonInstance", this);
    }

    public void doOperation() {
        //perform Singleton operation
    }
}
```

In this implementation, we use a static method called 'getInstance()'

to retrieve the Singleton instance. The 'getInstance()' method first checks if the Singleton instance is available in the distributed cache. If it is not available, a new instance is created, initialized, and saved to the cache. If the instance is available, it is retrieved from the cache.

The 'initialize()' method is used to perform any initialization tasks required for the Singleton instance. The 'doOperation()' method is used to perform the operation that the Singleton is designed for.

Note that the code relies on the assumption that the Singleton constructor is private. This is required to prevent users from creating multiple instances of the Singleton object.

In conclusion, we can achieve a Singleton instance across multiple servers in a distributed system by using a centralized mechanism for creating, storing, and accessing the instance. Using a distributed cache like Apache Ignite is one way to achieve this.

4.2 Discuss the impact of using Abstract Factory and Factory Method patterns on the overall testability of an application.

Abstract Factory and Factory Method patterns are creational patterns that encapsulate the creation of objects. They are widely used in software design as they provide a way to create objects without exposing the instantiation logic to the client. These patterns can have a significant impact on the testability of an application. In this answer, we will discuss the impact of using these patterns on the overall testability of an application.

Abstract Factory Pattern

The Abstract Factory pattern provides an interface for creating related objects without specifying their concrete classes. This pattern is used when we need to create families of related objects, and we want to isolate the client code from the implementation details of the objects. The Abstract Factory pattern involves creating an abstract factory interface and multiple concrete factory classes that implement this interface.

Using the Abstract Factory pattern can improve the testability of an application in the following ways:

- **Encapsulation of object creation logic:** The Abstract Factory pattern encapsulates the creation of objects, which allows us to easily mock the factory interfaces and substitute them with test doubles during unit testing. This makes it easier to test the client code independently of the concrete implementations of the objects.

- **Improvement of maintainability:** The Abstract Factory pattern allows us to change the implementation of the concrete factories without affecting the client code. This makes it easier to modify the application's behavior and fix bugs without breaking existing tests.

- **Reduction of code duplication:** By creating families of related objects using the Abstract Factory pattern, we can avoid duplicating the code for object creation in multiple places. This not only decreases the amount of code required, but it also reduces the likelihood of bugs arising from inconsistencies between object creation.

Here is an example of how the Abstract Factory pattern can be used to improve the testability of an application:

```java
public interface AnimalFactory {
    Animal createDog();
    Animal createCat();
}

public class DomesticAnimalFactory implements AnimalFactory {
    public Animal createDog() {
        return new DomesticDog();
    }

    public Animal createCat() {
        return new DomesticCat();
    }
}

public class WildAnimalFactory implements AnimalFactory {
    public Animal createDog() {
        return new WildDog();
    }

    public Animal createCat() {
        return new WildCat();
    }
}

public class AnimalShelter {
    private AnimalFactory factory;

    public AnimalShelter(AnimalFactory factory) {
        this.factory = factory;
    }

    public void adoptDog() {
        Animal dog = factory.createDog();
        // ...
    }

    public void adoptCat() {
        Animal cat = factory.createCat();
        // ...
    }

    // ...
}
```

In the example above, the AnimalShelter class depends on the abstract AnimalFactory interface, which allows us to easily substitute the concrete factories with test doubles during unit testing. The concrete factories encapsulate the logic for creating related objects, and any changes to the implementation of the factories won't affect the client code.

Factory Method Pattern

The Factory Method pattern defines an interface for creating objects, but it allows the subclasses to decide which class to instantiate. This pattern is used when we need to create objects in a subclass-specific manner. The Factory Method pattern involves creating an abstract creator class and multiple concrete creator subclasses that implement this class.

Using the Factory Method pattern can improve the testability of an application in the following ways:

- **Encapsulation of object creation logic:** The Factory Method pattern encapsulates the creation of objects, which allows us to easily mock the creator interfaces and substitute them with test doubles during unit testing. This makes it easier to test the client code independently of the concrete implementations of the objects.

- **Improvement of maintainability:** The Factory Method pattern allows us to change the implementation of the concrete creators without affecting the client code. This makes it easier to modify the application's behavior and fix bugs without breaking existing tests.

- **Reduction of code duplication:** By providing an interface for object creation logic in the creator classes, we can avoid duplicating the code for object creation in multiple places. This not only decreases the amount of code required, but it also

reduces the likelihood of bugs arising from inconsistencies between object creation.

Here is an example of how the Factory Method pattern can be
used to improve the testability of an application:

```
public interface AnimalFactory {
    Animal createAnimal();
}

public class DogFactory implements AnimalFactory {
    public Animal createAnimal() {
        return new Dog();
    }
}

public class CatFactory implements AnimalFactory {
    public Animal createAnimal() {
        return new Cat();
    }
}

public class AnimalShelter {
    private AnimalFactory factory;

    public AnimalShelter(AnimalFactory factory) {
        this.factory = factory;
    }

    public void adoptAnimal() {
        Animal animal = factory.createAnimal();
        // ...
    }

    // ...
}
```

In the example above, the AnimalShelter class depends on the
abstract AnimalFactory interface, which allows us to easily substitute the concrete factories with test doubles during unit testing. The concrete factories encapsulate the logic for creating
related objects, and any changes to the implementation of the
factories won't affect the client code.

In conclusion, both Abstract Factory and Factory Method patterns provide a way to encapsulate object creation logic and improve the testability of an application by allowing us to substitute the concrete implementations of the factories with test doubles during unit testing. These patterns also improve maintainability and reduce code duplication, which leads to fewer bugs and easier modification of the application's behavior.

4.3   Explain how you would handle data consistency and race conditions in an Observer pattern implementation.

Observer pattern is a widely used software design pattern that is used to maintain a one-to-many dependency between objects, such that whenever the state of one object changes, all its dependents are notified and updated automatically. However, when implementing an Observer pattern, one of the main challenges is handling data consistency and race conditions that may arise when multiple objects are trying to update and access the same data concurrently.

To handle data consistency and race conditions in an Observer pattern implementation, there are several techniques that can be used, including:

1. Synchronization: One of the most common ways of handling data consistency and race conditions in an Observer pattern implementation is to use synchronization. This involves using locks to ensure that only one thread can access and modify the data at any given time. In Java, synchronization can be achieved using the 'synchronized' keyword, which can be applied to methods or blocks of code:

```
public synchronized void update(int value) {
    // update the data here
}
```

2. Atomic operations: Another technique for handling data consistency and race conditions is to use atomic operations. Atomic operations are operations that are guaranteed to be executed as a single, indivisible operation, without any interference from other threads. In Java, atomic operations can be achieved using the 'java.util.concurrent.atomic' package, which provides classes such as 'AtomicInteger', 'AtomicBoolean', and 'AtomicReference'.

```
private final AtomicInteger count = new AtomicInteger(0);

public void update() {
    // increment the count atomically
    count.incrementAndGet();
}
```

3. Immutable objects: Another approach to handling data consistency and race conditions is to use immutable objects. Immutable objects are objects that cannot be modified once they are created. By using immutable objects, we can avoid the need for synchronization or atomic operations altogether, since there is no risk of data inconsistency or race conditions.

```
public class ImmutableData {
    private final int value;

    public ImmutableData(int value) {
        this.value = value;
    }

    public int getValue() {
        return value;
    }
}

public void update(ImmutableData data) {
    // create a new immutable data object with the updated value
    data = new ImmutableData(data.getValue() + 1);
}
```

In conclusion, when implementing an Observer pattern, it is important to consider the issues of data consistency and race conditions that may arise. By using techniques such as synchronization, atomic operations, or immutable objects, we can ensure that our implementation is robust and reliable, and that all updates to the data are performed correctly and without interference from other threads.

4.4   How would you design a Decorator pattern implementation to ensure type safety and avoid runtime type errors?

The Decorator pattern is a structural design pattern that allows behavior to be added to an individual object, either statically or dynamically, without affecting the behavior of other objects from the same class. It is frequently used to achieve a robust design that accommodates numerous enhancements or modifications over time.

When implementing the Decorator pattern in Java, it's crucial to ensure that the program is type-safe and free of runtime type errors. Here are some design guidelines for this purpose:

1. Define an abstract class or interface that specifies the basic functionality that will be decorated. This class should be type-safe and provide a clear definition of the methods that need to be implemented by the concrete decorators. It is important to note that all decorators and the concrete components should implement this interface.

```
public interface Component {
    public void operation();
```

```
}
```

2. Create a concrete implementation of the interface or abstract class for the base component.

```
public class ConcreteComponent implements Component {
    public void operation() {
        System.out.println("ConcreteComponent.operation()");
    }
}
```

3. Create a decorator class that has a reference to a Component object (usually set through the constructor). This class should extend the Component interface to ensure type safety.

```
public abstract class Decorator implements Component {
    protected Component component;
    public Decorator(Component component) {
        this.component = component;
    }
    public void operation() {
        component.operation();
    }
}
```

4. Create concrete decorator classes that add behavior to the basic component. Each decorator should take in a Component instance in its constructor and call its parent constructor with that instance to ensure the reference is stored appropriately. By treating the Component as an instance variable, each concrete decorator can preserve its own state and avoid changing the behavior of others.

```
public class ConcreteDecoratorA extends Decorator {
    private String addedState;
    public ConcreteDecoratorA(Component component) {
        super(component);
    }
    public void operation() {
        super.operation();
        addedState = "New_State";
        System.out.println("ConcreteDecoratorA.operation()");
    }
```

```
}
public class ConcreteDecoratorB extends Decorator {
    public ConcreteDecoratorB(Component component) {
        super(component);
    }
    public void operation() {
        super.operation();
        addedBehavior();
        System.out.println("ConcreteDecoratorB.operation()");
    }
    private void addedBehavior() {
        // ...
    }
}
```

5. Use the components and decorators correctly to create desired composite objects. For instance, to add decorators to a
ConcreteComponent decorator chain, they should be chained
like so:

"' Component component = new ConcreteDecoratorB(new Con-
creteDecoratorA(new ConcreteComponent())); component.op-
eration(); "'

This implementation will ensure that the objects being decorated are always of the correct type, and that any decorators
added will preserve the integrity of the type system, thus minimizing runtime type errors.

4.5   In which situations would you consider using the Strategy pattern over the State pattern for managing context-specific behavior?

The Strategy pattern and the State pattern are two design patterns that provide solutions for managing context-specific behaviors.

The Strategy pattern allows us to select an algorithm at runtime. It defines a family of algorithms, encapsulates each one, and makes them interchangeable. It enables us to vary the behavior of an object by providing a set of interchangeable algorithms or strategies. The main aim of the Strategy pattern is to provide a way to define a family of algorithms, encapsulate each one as an object, and make them interchangeable.

The State pattern, on the other hand, allows an object to alter its behavior when its internal state changes. It defines the state of an object, encapsulates state-specific behavior, and provides a mechanism to switch between states. This pattern enables an object to change its behavior when its internal state changes. The State pattern is useful when an object's behavior depends on its internal state, and the behavior changes when the state changes.

When deciding between the use of the Strategy pattern and the State pattern for managing context-specific behavior, the following factors should be considered:

1. Dynamic behavior change: If the behavior of an object can change dynamically during runtime, the Strategy pattern is

more suitable. The Strategy pattern provides a flexible solution for dynamic behavior change as we can swap strategies at runtime.

2. Multiple states: If an object has a finite number of states, and its behavior depends on its current state, the State pattern is more suitable. The State pattern provides a clean and maintainable solution to handle state-specific behavior.

3. Code complexity: The State pattern generally leads to more complex code because it involves managing a larger number of classes. On the other hand, the Strategy pattern involves managing a smaller number of classes and is generally simpler to implement.

4. Code reuse: The Strategy pattern is beneficial when dealing with multiple objects to perform the same operation but with different behaviors. We can reuse strategies across different objects. The State pattern is useful when dealing with hierarchical state transitions, and the same state transitions occur between different objects.

To illustrate the difference between the two patterns, let's consider an example where we want to implement a media player that can play different media types. We can use the Strategy pattern to encapsulate different media players' playback strategies for each media type, and at runtime, we can switch to the playback strategy for the desired media type. In contrast, with the State pattern, we can encapsulate the media player's behavior in different states, such as the playing state, paused state, and stopped state. When the user interacts with the media player, we can transition between different states and update the behavior accordingly.

Here's a simple implementation of the Strategy pattern where
we have different playback strategies for different media types:

```java
public interface MediaPlaybackStrategy {
  void play(Media media);
}

public class AudioPlaybackStrategy implements MediaPlaybackStrategy
    {
  @Override
  public void play(Media media) {
    // Play audio media
  }
}

public class VideoPlaybackStrategy implements MediaPlaybackStrategy
    {
  @Override
  public void play(Media media) {
    // Play video media
  }
}

public class MediaPlayer {
  private MediaPlaybackStrategy strategy;

  public void setPlaybackStrategy(MediaPlaybackStrategy strategy) {
    this.strategy = strategy;
  }

  public void play(Media media) {
    strategy.play(media);
  }
}
```

Here's a simple implementation of the State pattern where we
have different states for a media player:

```java
public interface MediaPlayerState {
  void play();
  void pause();
  void stop();
}

public class PlayingState implements MediaPlayerState {
  private final MediaPlayer mediaPlayer;

  public PlayingState(MediaPlayer mediaPlayer) {
    this.mediaPlayer = mediaPlayer;
  }

  @Override
```

```java
    public void play() {
      // No-op
    }

    @Override
    public void pause() {
      mediaPlayer.setState(new PausedState(mediaPlayer));
    }

    @Override
    public void stop() {
      mediaPlayer.setState(new StoppedState(mediaPlayer));
    }
}

public class PausedState implements MediaPlayerState {
    private final MediaPlayer mediaPlayer;

    public PausedState(MediaPlayer mediaPlayer) {
      this.mediaPlayer = mediaPlayer;
    }

    @Override
    public void play() {
      mediaPlayer.setState(new PlayingState(mediaPlayer));
    }

    @Override
    public void pause() {
      // No-op
    }

    @Override
    public void stop() {
      mediaPlayer.setState(new StoppedState(mediaPlayer));
    }
}

public class StoppedState implements MediaPlayerState {
    private final MediaPlayer mediaPlayer;

    public StoppedState(MediaPlayer mediaPlayer) {
      this.mediaPlayer = mediaPlayer;
    }

    @Override
    public void play() {
      mediaPlayer.setState(new PlayingState(mediaPlayer));
    }

    @Override
    public void pause() {
      // No-op
    }

    @Override
```

```
   public void stop() {
      // No-op
   }
}

public class MediaPlayer {
   private MediaPlayerState state;

   public void setState(MediaPlayerState state) {
      this.state = state;
   }

   public void play() {
      state.play();
   }

   public void pause() {
      state.pause();
   }

   public void stop() {
      state.stop();
   }
}
```

In conclusion, choosing between the Strategy pattern and the State pattern for managing context-specific behavior depends on the specific requirements of the system. If behavior changes dynamically during runtime, or the need for code reuse is high, the Strategy pattern is more suitable. But if an object has a finite number of states or we want to handle complex hierarchical state transitions, the State pattern is more appropriate.

4.6   Describe how you can combine the State pattern with the Flyweight pattern to optimize memory usage in a large state machine.

The State pattern is a behavioral design pattern that allows an object to alter its behavior when its internal state changes. The Flyweight pattern, on the other hand, is a structural design pattern that allows sharing objects to support large numbers of fine-grained objects with a minimal memory footprint.

When working with a large state machine using the State pattern, we can take advantage of the Flyweight pattern to optimize memory usage. We can create a shared pool of State objects that can be reused by different contexts. This shared pool of State objects is known as the flyweight objects and can drastically reduce the memory footprint of the state machine.

To implement this optimization, we can update the Context class to use a Flyweight factory instead of creating new State objects every time its state changes. The Flyweight factory will maintain a pool of flyweight objects and will return an existing object if available, or create a new object if necessary. Each flyweight object will contain only the state-specific data, while the state machine's Context class will store the non-state-specific data.

Here is an example implementation in Java:

First, we define the State interface, which contains the common behavior of all states.

```
public interface State {
```

```
    void performAction(Context context);
}
```

Next, we implement the ConcreteStateA and ConcreteStateB classes that represent specific states.

```
public class ConcreteStateA implements State {
    @Override
    public void performAction(Context context) {
        // perform action for state A
        // update state if necessary
        context.setState(/** new state **/);
    }
}

public class ConcreteStateB implements State {
    @Override
    public void performAction(Context context) {
        // perform action for state B
        // update state if necessary
        context.setState(/** new state **/);
    }
}
```

We then update the Context class to use the Flyweight factory to manage states.

```
public class Context {
    private State currentState;
    private FlyweightFactory flyweightFactory;

    public Context() {
        flyweightFactory = new FlyweightFactory();
        currentState = flyweightFactory.getState(/** initial state *
            */);
    }

    public void performAction() {
        currentState.performAction(this);
    }

    public void setState(State state) {
        currentState = flyweightFactory.getState(state);
    }
}
```

Finally, we implement the FlyweightFactory class to create and manage flyweight objects.

```
public class FlyweightFactory {
    private Map<State, State> flyweights = new HashMap<>();

    public State getState(State state) {
        if (!flyweights.containsKey(state)) {
            flyweights.put(state, state);
        }
        return flyweights.get(state);
    }
}
```

By using the Flyweight pattern in conjunction with the State pattern, we can reduce the memory footprint of a large state machine and optimize its performance.

4.7 When working with legacy systems, what challenges might you face when introducing the Adapter pattern, and how would you address them?

The Adapter pattern is used to convert an interface of a class into another interface that the client expects. When introducing the Adapter pattern to a legacy system, there may be some challenges that arise. In particular, there may be issues with backwards compatibility, adapting to existing code, and implementing the required functionality.

Backwards compatibility is a major concern when introducing any new pattern to a legacy system. Introducing the Adapter pattern may require changes to the existing system, which could break other parts of the code. To address this issue, it is important to thoroughly test the new implementation to ensure that it does not interfere with the existing system.

Another challenge with introducing the Adapter pattern to a
legacy system is adapting to the existing code. The legacy
codebase may not have been designed with the Adapter pattern in mind, and retrofitting the existing code to implement
the pattern may be difficult or impossible. In these cases,
it may be necessary to refactor the existing code to make it
more amenable to the Adapter pattern. This can be a time-
consuming process, but ultimately it can make the code more
maintainable and extensible in the long run.

Finally, implementing the required functionality can be challenging when introducing the Adapter pattern. The Adapter
must provide the same functionality as the original interface,
but in a different way. It may be necessary to use specialized libraries or frameworks to achieve the desired functionality, which
could lead to added complexity and potential risks.

To address these challenges, it is important to take a step-by-
step approach to introducing the Adapter pattern. Start by
identifying the areas of the legacy system that would benefit
from the pattern, and then work to refactor or reimplement
those areas in a way that is compatible with the Adapter pattern. Use testing and monitoring tools to identify any issues
that arise and address them promptly. Finally, document the
changes made to the system to ensure that other developers can
understand and maintain the codebase.

Here is an example implementation of the Adapter Pattern in
Java:

```java
public interface Target {
    public void request();
}
```

```
public class Adaptee {
   public void specificRequest() {
      System.out.println("Specific request");
   }
}

public class Adapter implements Target {
   private Adaptee adaptee;

   public Adapter(Adaptee adaptee) {
      this.adaptee = adaptee;
   }

   public void request() {
      adaptee.specificRequest();
   }
}
```

In this example, the 'Target' interface represents the interface that the client expects to interact with, whereas the 'Adaptee' represents the legacy interface that needs to be adapted. The 'Adapter' class implements the 'Target' interface and takes an instance of 'Adaptee' as a constructor parameter. The 're-quest()' method of the 'Adapter' class calls the 'specificRe-quest()' method of the 'Adaptee' instance, effectively adapting the legacy interface to the new interface. Following this example, one should carefully consider the needs of the system and utilize the Adapter pattern as a solution to the challenges and constraints faced in the development process.

4.8 How can you apply the Command pattern in a message-based architecture to support different message types and their processing?

In a message-based architecture, messages are the primary means of communication between various components of the system. These messages can be of different types and may require different processing methods. To support such a system, one can apply the Command pattern.

The Command pattern encapsulates a request or an operation as an object allowing us to parameterize clients with different requests, queue or log requests, and support undoable operations. In a message-based architecture, each message can be represented as a Command object. The Command object contains all the necessary information about the message, including the message type, sender, receiver, and the data payload.

To support different message types and their processing, we can define an interface called 'Command' that defines a single method called 'execute'. The 'Command' interface can be implemented by different message processor classes, each responsible for processing a specific message type. Each processor class can take the message payload as a constructor argument, and its 'execute' method can implement the processing logic for that message type.

Here's an example implementation in Java:

```java
// Command interface for different message types
public interface Command {
    void execute();
}
```

```java
// Concrete command implementation for message of type "Email"
public class EmailCommand implements Command {
    private String from;
    private String to;
    private String subject;
    private String content;

    public EmailCommand(String from, String to, String subject,
        String content) {
        this.from = from;
        this.to = to;
        this.subject = subject;
        this.content = content;
    }

    @Override
    public void execute() {
        //processing logic for email message
        System.out.println("Sending email from " + from + " to " + to
            + ", Subject: " + subject + ", Content: " + content);
    }
}

// Concrete command implementation for message of type "SMS"
public class SMSCommand implements Command {
    private String from;
    private String to;
    private String content;

    public SMSCommand(String from, String to, String content) {
        this.from = from;
        this.to = to;
        this.content = content;
    }

    @Override
    public void execute() {
        //processing logic for SMS message
        System.out.println("Sending SMS from " + from + " to " + to +
            ", Content: " + content);
    }
}


// Invoker class that receives the message and invokes corresponding
    command to process it.
public class MessageProcessor {
    private Command command;

    public void receiveMessage(Command command) {
        this.command = command;
        this.command.execute();
    }
}

// Client code - the message sender
```

```
public class Client {
   public static void main(String[] args) {
      // create message commands
      Command emailCommand = new EmailCommand("user1@gmail.com", "
         user2@gmail.com", "Test Email", "Hello from user 1!");
      Command smsCommand = new SMSCommand("1234567890", "0987654321
         ", "Hello from user 1!");

      // create message processor and send messages
      MessageProcessor processor = new MessageProcessor();
      processor.receiveMessage(emailCommand);
      processor.receiveMessage(smsCommand);
   }
}
```

In this example, the 'Command' interface defines a single method called 'execute', which is implemented by the concrete command classes such as 'EmailCommand' and 'SMSCommand'. The 'MessageProcessor' class acts as the invoker, accepting the specific command as input and invoking its 'execute' method to process the message. Finally, the 'Client' class creates the appropriate message commands and sends them to the message processor for execution.

By using the Command pattern, we have a flexible and extensible system that can handle different message types with varying processing needs. We can easily add new message types and their corresponding processing logic by creating new concrete command classes and implementing the 'Command' interface.

4.9   Explain the differences between the Prototype pattern and the Object Pool pattern, and discuss the use cases for each.

The Prototype pattern and the Object Pool pattern are both creational design patterns, but they differ in their purposes and use cases. The Prototype pattern provides an efficient way to create new objects by cloning existing ones, while the Object Pool pattern manages a pool of reusable objects that can be shared among multiple clients.

Prototype Pattern

The Prototype pattern is used when creating a new object has a high overhead cost or when creating a deep clone of an existing object is required. In this pattern, we create a prototype object and then create new objects by cloning the prototype. This can be done using a shallow or a deep copy, depending on the requirements.

The Prototype pattern can be implemented in Java using the 'clone()' method, which creates a copy of the object. However, this method requires the 'Cloneable' interface to be implemented and the 'clone()' method to be overridden. Alternatively, libraries like Apache Commons provide a 'CloneUtils' class that can be used to clone objects.

```
public class PrototypePatternExample {
  public static void main(String[] args) {
    Circle circle = new Circle(10, 20, 5);
    Circle clonedCircle = (Circle) circle.clone();
  }
}
```

```
class Circle implements Cloneable {
  private int x, y, radius;

  public Circle(int x, int y, int radius) {
    this.x = x;
    this.y = y;
    this.radius = radius;
  }

  public Circle clone() {
    try {
      return (Circle) super.clone();
    } catch (CloneNotSupportedException e) {
      e.printStackTrace();
      return null;
    }
  }
}
```

Object Pool Pattern

The Object Pool pattern is used when the creation of new objects is expensive and reuse of objects is beneficial. This pattern maintains a pool of objects that can be shared among multiple clients to avoid the overhead cost of creating new objects. Objects in the pool are available for clients to use and are returned to the pool when they are no longer needed.

In Java, the Object Pool pattern can be implemented using the 'java.util.concurrent' package, which provides a 'BlockingQueue' interface. Clients can request objects from the pool using the 'take()' method, and objects can be returned to the pool using the 'put()' method.

```
public class ObjectPoolExample {
  public static void main(String[] args) {
    ObjectPool pool = new ObjectPool();
    Object object1 = pool.getObject();
    Object object2 = pool.getObject();
    pool.returnObject(object1);
  }
}
class ObjectPool {
  private BlockingQueue<Object> pool;
```

```
public ObjectPool() {
  pool = new LinkedBlockingQueue<>();
  pool.add(new Object());
  pool.add(new Object());
  pool.add(new Object());
}

public Object getObject() {
  try {
    return pool.take();
  } catch (InterruptedException e) {
    e.printStackTrace();
    return null;
  }
}

public void returnObject(Object object) {
  pool.add(object);
}
}
```

In summary, the Prototype pattern is used to create new objects efficiently by cloning existing ones, while the Object Pool pattern is used to manage a pool of reusable objects that can be shared among multiple clients.

4.10   Discuss the pros and cons of using the Builder pattern with a Director class to control the object creation process.

The Builder pattern is a creational design pattern that separates the construction of a complex object from its representation, allowing the same construction process to create different representations. The Director class is an optional component of the pattern that controls the object creation process by invoking the appropriate Builder methods.

Pros of using the Builder pattern with a Director class:

1. Encapsulation: The Builder pattern encapsulates the creation and assembly of complex objects, making the code more modular and easier to modify. The Director class further encapsulates the creation process by separating the construction logic from the client code.

2. Flexibility: The Builder pattern allows the same construction process to create different representations of an object, which can be useful when dealing with complex or evolving requirements. The Director class provides a way to change the construction process dynamically, without modifying the client code.

3. Reusability: The Builder pattern makes it easy to reuse the same construction process to create multiple instances of similar or related objects. The Director class can be reused with different Builder implementations to create different configurations of the same object.

4. Complexity management: The Builder pattern can simplify the management of complex object creation logic by breaking it down into smaller, more manageable pieces. The Director class can coordinate the steps of the construction process, hiding the details from the client code.

Cons of using the Builder pattern with a Director class:

1. Overhead: The Builder pattern can introduce extra overhead and complexity to the code, especially when dealing with simple objects or small projects. The Director class can add another layer of abstraction, making the code harder to read and understand.

2. Coupling: The Builder pattern can increase coupling between the Builder and Director classes, making it harder to modify them independently. Changes to the Builder interface or implementation can affect the Director class, and vice versa.

3. Limited extensibility: The Builder pattern is not very extensible, as adding new features or properties to the object can require modifying the Builder interface and all its implementations. The Director class can also be limited in its extensibility, as it may not be able to handle new types of Builders without modification.

4. Code duplication: The Builder pattern can lead to code duplication, as each Builder implementation needs to implement the same set of methods. The Director class can also duplicate code if it needs to handle multiple types of Builders with similar construction logic.

Here's an example of using the Builder pattern with a Director class in Java:

```java
public interface Builder {
    void buildPartA();
    void buildPartB();
    void buildPartC();
    Product getResult();
}

public class ConcreteBuilder implements Builder {
    private Product product = new Product();

    public void buildPartA() {
        // build Part A of the product
        product.setPartA(...);
    }

    public void buildPartB() {
        // build Part B of the product
        product.setPartB(...);
    }

    public void buildPartC() {
```

```
        // build Part C of the product
        product.setPartC(...);
    }

    public Product getResult() {
        return product;
    }
}

public class Director {
    private Builder builder;

    public Director(Builder builder) {
        this.builder = builder;
    }

    public void construct() {
        builder.buildPartA();
        builder.buildPartB();
        builder.buildPartC();
    }
}
```

In this example, the Builder interface defines methods for building different parts of the product, and for returning the final object. The ConcreteBuilder implements the Builder interface, and provides implementations for each method. The Director class takes a Builder object as a parameter, and coordinates the construction process by invoking the Builder methods in a specific order.

Overall, the Builder pattern with a Director class can be a useful approach for managing complex object creation logic, but it may not be necessary or appropriate for all projects. Developers should carefully consider the trade-offs before using this pattern, and use it only when it provides clear benefits over simpler alternatives.

4.11 Explain how you can use the Facade pattern to create a versioned API while maintaining backward compatibility.

The Facade design pattern provides a simplified interface to a more complex underlying system, hiding its complexities from the client code. In the context of an API, a facade can be used to simplify the usage of that API for the client code.

To create a versioned API while maintaining backward compatibility using the Facade pattern, we can have a separate facade implementation for each version of the API. Each facade implementation can encapsulate the corresponding version of the API, allowing the client code to use the new version without breaking the existing code.

Let's see an example of how this can be achieved in Java:

Suppose we have an API for a weather forecasting service, which has two versions, v1 and v2. We can create two facade implementations, WeatherServiceFacadeV1 and WeatherServiceFacadeV2, each implementing a simplified interface for its corresponding version of the API. We can make sure that both facades have the same public methods or methods which can provide the same functionality with different implementation versions.

```
public interface WeatherService {
    Weather getWeather(String location, LocalDate date);
}

public class WeatherServiceV1 implements WeatherService {
    // implementation for version 1 of the API
}
```

```
public class WeatherServiceV2 implements WeatherService {
    // implementation for version 2 of the API
}

public class WeatherServiceFacadeV1 {
    private WeatherService weatherService;

    public WeatherServiceFacadeV1() {
        weatherService = new WeatherServiceV1();
    }

    public WeatherData getWeather(String location, String date) {
        // implementation using the WeatherServiceV1 implementation
    }
}

public class WeatherServiceFacadeV2 {
    private WeatherService weatherService;

    public WeatherServiceFacadeV2() {
        weatherService = new WeatherServiceV2();
    }

    public WeatherData getWeather(String location, LocalDate date) {
        // implementation using the WeatherServiceV2 implementation
    }
}
```

Now, the client code can use either of the facade implementations, depending on the version of the API it is using. For example:

```
WeatherServiceFacadeV1 weatherServiceFacadeV1 = new
    WeatherServiceFacadeV1();
WeatherData weatherDataV1 = weatherServiceFacadeV1.getWeather("
    London", "2022-11-25");

WeatherServiceFacadeV2 weatherServiceFacadeV2 = new
    WeatherServiceFacadeV2();
WeatherData weatherDataV2 = weatherServiceFacadeV2.getWeather("
    London", LocalDate.of(2022, 11, 25));
```

Thus, we can create different versions of the facade implementations for different versions of the API, making it easier for the client code to use the API without being affected by the changes in the API that might break the backward compatibility of the client code with the new version of the API.

4.12   How can you implement the Chain of Responsibility pattern in an asynchronous environment to handle requests with long processing times?

The Chain of Responsibility pattern is a behavioral design pattern that allows an object to pass a request along a chain of handlers until one of the handlers processes the request. In an asynchronous environment, requests with long processing times can cause delays, blocking, and resource consumption, which can negatively impact system performance and user experience. To address these challenges, the Chain of Responsibility pattern can be modified to handle requests asynchronously by using the Reactor pattern.

The Reactor pattern is a design pattern that handles I/O requests asynchronously by using an event loop, which dispatches events to their handlers. The event loop continuously checks for new events and dispatches them to the appropriate handler, allowing the application to handle multiple requests concurrently.

To implement the Chain of Responsibility pattern with the Reactor pattern, you can use a series of handlers, where each handler processes a specific type of request asynchronously. When a request is received, the first handler in the chain processes the request asynchronously and passes it to the next handler in the chain. If the request is not processed by any handler, the system returns an error message.

Here is an example of how you could implement the Chain of Responsibility pattern with the Reactor pattern in Java:

```
interface Handler {
```

```java
    boolean canHandle(Request request);
    void handle(Request request, Callback callback);
}

class Handler1 implements Handler {
    boolean canHandle(Request request) {
        return request.getType() == Type.TYPE1;
    }

    void handle(Request request, Callback callback) {
        // Process request asynchronously
        asyncProcess(request, result -> {
            if (result.isSuccessful()) {
                callback.onSuccess(result);
            } else {
                callback.onError(result.getError());
            }
        });
    }
}

class Handler2 implements Handler {
    boolean canHandle(Request request) {
        return request.getType() == Type.TYPE2;
    }

    void handle(Request request, Callback callback) {
        // Process request asynchronously
        asyncProcess(request, result -> {
            if (result.isSuccessful()) {
                callback.onSuccess(result);
            } else {
                callback.onError(result.getError());
            }
        });
    }
}

class Chain {
    private List<Handler> handlers;

    Chain() {
        handlers = new ArrayList<>();
        handlers.add(new Handler1());
        handlers.add(new Handler2());
    }

    void process(Request request, Callback callback) {
        Handler handler = findHandler(request);
        if (handler != null) {
            handler.handle(request, callback);
        } else {
            callback.onError(new Error("No handler found"));
```

```
        }
    }

    private Handler findHandler(Request request) {
        for (Handler handler : handlers) {
            if (handler.canHandle(request)) {
                return handler;
            }
        }
        return null;
    }
}

class Reactor {
    private Chain chain;

    Reactor() {
        chain = new Chain();
    }

    void dispatch(Request request, Callback callback) {
        chain.process(request, callback);
    }
}

class Request {
}

interface Callback {
    void onSuccess(Result result);
    void onError(Error error);
}

class Result {
    boolean isSuccessful() {}
    Error getError() {}
}

class Error {
}
```

In this example, the 'Handler' interface defines the handlers for
each type of request. The 'canHandle' method checks if a handler can process a request, and the 'handle' method processes
the request asynchronously and invokes the callback when finished.

The 'Chain' class implements the Chain of Responsibility pattern and contains a list of handlers. When a request is re-

ceived, the 'process' method finds the first handler in the list that can handle the request and passes it to the handler's 'handle' method.

The 'Reactor' class implements the Reactor pattern and contains an instance of the 'Chain' class. The 'dispatch' method receives a request and a callback, and passes them to the 'Chain' class's 'process' method.

The 'Request' class represents a request. The 'Callback' interface defines methods for handling successful and error responses. The 'Result' class represents a response, and the 'Error' class represents an error message.

By combining the Chain of Responsibility and Reactor patterns, you can handle requests with long processing times asynchronously and concurrently, improving system performance and user experience.

4.13   Describe a scenario where you would use the Composite pattern and the Decorator pattern together to build a complex object hierarchy.

The Composite pattern is used to represent objects in a hierarchical structure, where objects can have other objects as children, forming a tree-like structure. On the other hand, the Decorator pattern is used to dynamically add behavior or features to an object at runtime, allowing for flexible and modular code.

Let's consider a scenario where we are building a music application that allows users to create playlists of songs, and also apply filters to those playlists. The application supports different types of playlists such as regular playlists, smart playlists, and radio playlists. Each playlist can contain a list of songs, and the smart playlist can filter songs based on user preferences.

To build this complex hierarchy of objects, we can use the Composite pattern to represent the playlists and their songs. We can create a base interface or abstract class called PlaylistComponent to represent both the playlist and individual songs. Here's an example:

```
public interface PlaylistComponent {
    void play();
    String getName();
}
```

The interface has two methods 'play()' to play the component, and 'getName()' to get the name of the component.

The 'Playlist' class represents the composite object that can have other 'PlaylistComponent' objects as children:

```
public class Playlist implements PlaylistComponent {
    private List<PlaylistComponent> components;
    private String name;

    public Playlist(String name) {
        this.name = name;
        components = new ArrayList<>();
    }

    public void addComponent(PlaylistComponent component) {
        components.add(component);
    }

    public void removeComponent(PlaylistComponent component) {
        components.remove(component);
    }

    @Override
    public void play() {
```

```
            System.out.println("Playing␣playlist␣" + name);
            for (PlaylistComponent component : components) {
                component.play();
            }
        }

        @Override
        public String getName() {
            return name;
        }
    }
```

The 'Playlist' class has a list of child components, and it implements the 'play()' and 'getName()' methods to play the playlist and get the name.

The 'Song' class represents the leaf object that does not have any child components:

```
public class Song implements PlaylistComponent {
    private String name;
    private String artist;
    private String album;

    public Song(String name, String artist, String album) {
        this.name = name;
        this.artist = artist;
        this.album = album;
    }

    @Override
    public void play() {
        System.out.println("Playing␣song␣" + name + "␣by␣" + artist +
                "␣from␣" + album);
    }

    @Override
    public String getName() {
        return name;
    }
}
```

The 'Song' class implements the 'play()' and 'getName()' methods to play the song and get the name.

Now, to add filters to the playlists, we can use the Decorator pattern. We can create a base decorator interface called

'PlaylistFilter':

```
public interface PlaylistFilter extends PlaylistComponent {
    List<PlaylistComponent> getFilteredChildren();
}
```

The interface has a 'getFilteredChildren()' method that returns a filtered list of child components.

We can create different types of filters that implement this interface, such as 'GenreFilter', 'ArtistFilter', and 'AlbumFilter'. Each filter class takes a 'PlaylistComponent' object and filters its child components based on some criteria.

Here's an example of the 'GenreFilter' class:

```
public class GenreFilter implements PlaylistFilter {
    private PlaylistComponent component;
    private String genre;

    public GenreFilter(PlaylistComponent component, String genre) {
        this.component = component;
        this.genre = genre;
    }

    @Override
    public void play() {
        component.play();
    }

    @Override
    public String getName() {
        return component.getName();
    }

    @Override
    public List<PlaylistComponent> getFilteredChildren() {
        List<PlaylistComponent> filtered = new ArrayList<>();
        for (PlaylistComponent child : component.getFilteredChildren
            ()) {
            if (child instanceof Song) {
                Song song = (Song) child;
                if (song.getGenre().equals(genre)) {
                    filtered.add(child);
                }
            } else {
                filtered.add(child);
            }
```

```
        }
        return filtered;
    }
}
```

The 'GenreFilter' class takes a 'PlaylistComponent' object and filters its child components based on the genre of the songs. The 'getFilteredChildren()' method returns a filtered list of child components.

To create a smart playlist with filters, we can create a 'Smart-Playlist' class that extends the 'Playlist' class and adds filtering behavior at runtime:

```
public class SmartPlaylist extends Playlist {
    private PlaylistFilter filter;

    public SmartPlaylist(String name, PlaylistFilter filter) {
        super(name);
        this.filter = filter;
    }

    @Override
    public void play() {
        System.out.println("Playing␣smart␣playlist␣" + getName());
        for (PlaylistComponent component : filter.getFilteredChildren
            ()) {
            component.play();
        }
    }
}
```

The 'SmartPlaylist' class extends the 'Playlist' class and overrides the 'play()' method to play the filtered child components instead of all child components.

Now, we can create a hierarchical object structure by combining 'Playlist' and 'Song' objects using the Composite pattern. We can also create a smart playlist object by decorating a 'Playlist' object with filters using the Decorator pattern:

```
Playlist playlist = new Playlist("Playlist");
```

```
playlist.addComponent(new Song("Song␣1", "Artist␣1", "Album␣1"));
playlist.addComponent(new Song("Song␣2", "Artist␣2", "Album␣2"));
playlist.addComponent(new Song("Song␣3", "Artist␣3", "Album␣3"));

PlaylistFilter genreFilter = new GenreFilter(playlist, "Rock");
Playlist smartPlaylist = new SmartPlaylist("SmartPlaylist",
    genreFilter);
smartPlaylist.play();
```

In conclusion, we can combine the Composite and Decorator patterns to build complex object hierarchies that are both flexible and modular. The Composite pattern allows us to create a tree-like structure of objects, and the Decorator pattern allows us to add behavior or features to those objects at runtime.

4.14   What are the potential pitfalls of using the Flyweight pattern with mutable shared objects, and how can you mitigate these risks?

The Flyweight design pattern is a structural pattern that helps reduce the memory footprint of an application by sharing common, immutable objects among multiple similar objects instead of creating new objects each time.

However, when using the Flyweight pattern with mutable shared objects, there are potential pitfalls that can arise. Here are some of them:

1. Inconsistency: When multiple objects share the same mutable object, any changes made to the mutable object will affect all the objects that share it. If one object changes the state of the shared object, other objects that are using it may see

inconsistent states. This can lead to unpredictability and bugs.

2. Synchronization: Since multiple objects can access the same shared mutable object, synchronization is needed to ensure thread safety. Without proper synchronization, concurrent calls to the shared mutable object can lead to race conditions and other synchronization bugs.

3. Memory leaks: The Flyweight pattern can cause memory leaks when the shared objects are not properly released. Since multiple objects reference the same shared mutable object, the object cannot be released until all the objects have finished using it.

To mitigate these risks, here are some approaches:

1. Immutable objects: Use only immutable objects for sharing among multiple objects. Immutable objects cannot be changed once created, so all objects that share them will always see the same state. This eliminates the risk of inconsistency and synchronization issues.

2. Thread-safe objects: If mutable objects must be shared, make sure they are thread-safe. Thread-safe objects can be accessed concurrently without the risk of race conditions and other synchronization issues.

3. Reference counting: Keep track of the number of objects that reference the shared mutable object. When the count reaches zero, the object can be safely released. This ensures that memory leaks do not occur.

Here's an example of how to use the Flyweight pattern with immutable objects in Java:

```java
public class Tree {
  private int x;
  private int y;
  private TreeType treeType; // shared immutable object

  public Tree(int x, int y, TreeType treeType) {
    this.x = x;
    this.y = y;
    this.treeType = treeType;
  }

  public void draw() {
    treeType.draw(x, y);
  }
}

public class TreeType {
  private String name;
  private String color;
  private String texture;

  public TreeType(String name, String color, String texture) {
    this.name = name;
    this.color = color;
    this.texture = texture;
  }

  public void draw(int x, int y) {
    System.out.println("Drawing a " + color + " " + texture + " " +
        name + " at (" + x + ", " + y + ")");
  }
}

public class Client {
  private static final Map<String, TreeType> treeTypes = new HashMap
      <>();

  public static void main(String[] args) {
    TreeType oakType = getTreeType("Oak", "Brown", "Textured");
    TreeType mapleType = getTreeType("Maple", "Red", "Smooth");

    Tree oak1 = new Tree(10, 20, oakType);
    Tree oak2 = new Tree(30, 40, oakType);
    Tree maple1 = new Tree(50, 60, mapleType);
    Tree maple2 = new Tree(70, 80, mapleType);

    oak1.draw(); // Drawing a Brown Textured Oak at (10, 20)
    oak2.draw(); // Drawing a Brown Textured Oak at (30, 40)
    maple1.draw(); // Drawing a Red Smooth Maple at (50, 60)
    maple2.draw(); // Drawing a Red Smooth Maple at (70, 80)
  }

  private static TreeType getTreeType(String name, String color,
      String texture) {
    TreeType treeType = treeTypes.get(name);
    if (treeType == null) {
```

```
        treeType = new TreeType(name, color, texture);
        treeTypes.put(name, treeType);
    }
    return treeType;
  }
}
```

In this example, the 'TreeType' class represents an immutable shared object that represents a type of tree. The 'draw' method of the 'Tree' class takes in a 'TreeType' object and calls its 'draw' method, which prints out the details of the tree. The 'Client' class demonstrates how to create multiple 'Tree' objects that share the same 'TreeType' objects.

By using immutable objects for sharing, this example eliminates the risk of inconsistency and synchronization issues.

4.15 Discuss the role of the Mediator pattern in implementing communication between microservices in an event-driven architecture.

In an event-driven architecture, microservices communicate with each other asynchronously by publishing and subscribing to events. Mediator pattern plays an important role in implementing communication between microservices in an event-driven architecture by providing a central point of communication and decoupling the microservices from each other.

The Mediator pattern promotes loose coupling by keeping objects from referring to each other explicitly, and it lets you vary their interaction independently. A mediator is a behavioral design pattern that lets you reduce chaotic dependencies between objects. The pattern restricts direct communications between the objects and forces them to collaborate only via a mediator object. This way, the objects can maintain their independence from each other while still exchange data.

In the context of microservices communication, the Mediator pattern can be implemented by introducing a Message Broker. A message broker is an intermediary service that acts as a communication channel for different microservices. A message broker receives messages from producers and routes them to the appropriate consumers. This way, the producers do not need to know about the consumers and vice versa, and they communicate with each other indirectly through the message broker.

The following Java code example demonstrates a simple Mediator pattern implementation using Spring Boot and RabbitMQ as the message broker:

```java
// Producer Microservice
@RestController
public class ProducerController {

    @Autowired
    private RabbitTemplate rabbitTemplate;

    @PostMapping("/event")
    public void sendMessage(@RequestBody Event event) {
        rabbitTemplate.convertAndSend("events.exchange", "events.key"
            , event);
    }
}

// Consumer Microservice
@Component
public class Consumer {

    @RabbitListener(queues = "events.queue")
    public void receiveMessage(Event event) {
        // process the event
    }
}

// RabbitMQ Configuration
```

```
@Configuration
public class RabbitMQConfig {

    @Bean
    public Queue queue() {
        return new Queue("events.queue", false);
    }

    @Bean
    public TopicExchange exchange() {
        return new TopicExchange("events.exchange");
    }

    @Bean
    public Binding binding(Queue queue, TopicExchange exchange) {
        return BindingBuilder.bind(queue).to(exchange).with("events.
            key");
    }

    @Bean
    public MessageConverter messageConverter() {
        return new Jackson2JsonMessageConverter();
    }

    @Bean
    public RabbitTemplate rabbitTemplate(ConnectionFactory
        connectionFactory) {
        RabbitTemplate rabbitTemplate = new RabbitTemplate(
            connectionFactory);
        rabbitTemplate.setMessageConverter(messageConverter());
        return rabbitTemplate;
    }
}
```

In the above code example, the Producer microservice uses Rab-
bitTemplate to publish an event to the "events.exchange" with
routing key "events.key". The Consumer microservice listens to
the "events.queue" and processes the event once it arrives. The
connection between the two microservices is established through
RabbitMQ acting as a mediator by receiving messages from the
Producer and routing them to the appropriate Consumer.

In conclusion, the Mediator pattern plays a crucial role in implementing communication between microservices in an event-
driven architecture by providing a central communication point
and decoupling the microservices from each other. By intro-

ducing a Message Broker as a mediator, each microservice can communicate with others indirectly and maintain independence while exchanging data.

4.16 How can you use the Proxy pattern to implement caching, and what challenges might you face in maintaining cache consistency?

The Proxy pattern allows us to provide a surrogate or placeholder for an object in order to control its access. Using the Proxy pattern, we can implement caching by creating a proxy object that serves as a cache for the actual object. When a client requests an object, the proxy checks if the object is available in the cache. If the object is found in the cache, the proxy returns the cached object without accessing the actual object. If the object is not found in the cache, the proxy retrieves it from the actual object, caches it, and then returns it to the client.

Here's an example of how we can use the Proxy pattern to implement caching in Java:

```java
public interface DataService {
    public List<String> getData();
}

public class DataServiceImpl implements DataService {
    public List<String> getData() {
        // code to retrieve data from a database or a web service
        // ...
    }
}

public class DataProxy implements DataService {
    private DataService actualService;
```

```
    private List<String> cachedData;

    public DataProxy(DataService actualService) {
        this.actualService = actualService;
    }

    public List<String> getData() {
        if (cachedData == null) {
            cachedData = actualService.getData();
        }
        return cachedData;
    }
}
```

In this example, we have an interface 'DataService' that defines the contract for retrieving data. We also have a concrete implementation 'DataServiceImpl' that retrieves data from a database or a web service. Finally, we have a proxy 'DataProxy' that implements the 'DataService' interface and maintains a cache of the retrieved data.

The 'DataProxy' constructor takes an object of the 'DataService' interface as a parameter, which we refer to as the actual service. The 'getData()' method first checks if the cached data is available. If the cached data is not available, the proxy requests the actual service to retrieve the data, caches the retrieved data, and returns it to the client. If the cached data is available, the proxy returns it directly to the client without accessing the actual service.

One of the challenges of using the Proxy pattern for caching is maintaining cache consistency. If the actual object changes, we need to invalidate the cached data to ensure that subsequent requests retrieve the updated data. One way to handle this is to set an expiration time for the cached data so that it is refreshed after a certain period of time. Another way is to use an event-driven approach to invalidate the cached data whenever the actual object changes.

```
public class DataProxy implements DataService {
    private DataService actualService;
    private List<String> cachedData;
    private long lastUpdate;

    public DataProxy(DataService actualService) {
        this.actualService = actualService;
        lastUpdate = 0;
    }

    public synchronized List<String> getData() {
        if (cachedData == null || System.currentTimeMillis() -
            lastUpdate > CACHE_EXPIRATION_TIME) {
            cachedData = actualService.getData();
            lastUpdate = System.currentTimeMillis();
        }
        return cachedData;
    }

    public synchronized void invalidateCache() {
        cachedData = null;
        lastUpdate = 0;
    }
}
```

In this modified example, we have added a 'lastUpdate' field
to keep track of the time when the data was last retrieved
from the actual service. The 'getData()' method now checks if
the cached data has expired based on the 'CACHE_EXPIRA-
TION_TIME' constant, and if it has, retrieves the data from
the actual service, caches it, and updates 'lastUpdate'.

We have also added a new 'invalidateCache()' method that in-
validates the cached data by setting it to 'null' and resetting
'lastUpdate' to '0'. This method can be called whenever the actual object changes to ensure that subsequent requests retrieve
the updated data.

In summary, we can use the Proxy pattern to implement caching
by creating a proxy object that caches the retrieved data from
the actual object. However, we need to be careful to maintain cache consistency by either setting an expiration time or
using an event-driven approach to invalidate the cached data

whenever the actual object changes.

4.17   Describe a scenario where using the Bridge pattern with the Adapter pattern can help solve complex integration problems.

The Bridge pattern is a structural design pattern that allows us to split a large class or a set of closely related classes into two separate hierarchies: abstraction and implementation. The Adapter pattern is also a structural pattern that allows us to modify the interface of an existing class so that it matches what a client expects.

Often, when dealing with complex integration problems, we have to work with multiple systems, each with its own data model and interfaces. In such scenarios, using the Bridge pattern with the Adapter pattern can be helpful in solving complex integration problems.

For instance, let's consider a hypothetical scenario where we have two separate systems: a legacy payroll system and a modern HR system. Both systems store employee data, but they have different data models and interfaces. The legacy system stores employee data in CSV format, and the HR system stores employee data in JSON format.

To integrate these two systems and ensure that we can perform operations on the employee data such as creating, updating, and deleting records, we can use the Bridge pattern with the Adapter pattern in the following manner:

1. First, we create an abstraction hierarchy that defines the operations that we can perform on employee data. This may include operations such as creating a new employee record, updating an existing record, and deleting a record. We then create an implementation hierarchy that defines how employee data is stored and retrieved in each system. For example, we may have a CSV implementation class that reads and writes employee data to the legacy system and a JSON implementation class that reads and writes employee data to the modern HR system.

2. Next, we use the Adapter pattern to modify the interface of the CSV and JSON implementation classes so that they match the abstraction hierarchy. This allows us to perform the same operations on employee data regardless of which system it is stored in. For example, we can create a CSVAdapter and a JSONAdapter class that implement the same methods as the abstraction classes, but use the appropriate implementation classes for reading and writing data.

3. Finally, we can use the Bridge pattern to link the abstraction hierarchy with the implementation hierarchy, allowing us to switch between different implementation classes at runtime as needed. For example, we may have a PayrollSystem class that uses the CSV implementation for reading and writing employee data, and an HRSystem class that uses the JSON implementation. By linking the PayrollSystem and HRSystem classes with the appropriate abstraction classes using the Bridge pattern, we can perform operations on employee data regardless of which system it is stored in.

Here's an example Java code snippet that demonstrates how the Bridge pattern and Adapter pattern can be used together to integrate the two systems:

```
// Abstraction hierarchy
interface EmployeeData {
    void createEmployee(Employee employee);
    void updateEmployee(Employee employee);
    void deleteEmployee(int id);
}

// Implementation hierarchy
interface EmployeeDataImpl {
    List<Employee> getAllEmployees();
    Employee getEmployeeById(int id);
    void saveEmployee(Employee employee);
    void removeEmployee(Employee employee);
}

// CSV implementation
class CSVEmployeeDataImpl implements EmployeeDataImpl {
    // implementation details
}

// JSON implementation
class JSONEmployeeDataImpl implements EmployeeDataImpl {
    // implementation details
}

// Adapter for CSV implementation
class CSVEmployeeDataAdapter extends CSVEmployeeDataImpl implements
    EmployeeData {
    @Override
    public void createEmployee(Employee employee) {
        // implementation details
    }

    @Override
    public void updateEmployee(Employee employee) {
        // implementation details
    }

    @Override
    public void deleteEmployee(int id) {
        // implementation details
    }
}

// Adapter for JSON implementation
class JSONEmployeeDataAdapter extends JSONEmployeeDataImpl
    implements EmployeeData {
    @Override
    public void createEmployee(Employee employee) {
        // implementation details
    }

    @Override
    public void updateEmployee(Employee employee) {
```

```java
        // implementation details
    }

    @Override
    public void deleteEmployee(int id) {
        // implementation details
    }
}

// Bridge between abstraction and implementation hierarchies
class EmployeeManager {
    private EmployeeData employeeData;

    public EmployeeManager(EmployeeData employeeData) {
        this.employeeData = employeeData;
    }

    public List<Employee> getAllEmployees() {
        return employeeData.getAllEmployees();
    }

    public Employee getEmployeeById(int id) {
        return employeeData.getEmployeeById(id);
    }

    public void createEmployee(Employee employee) {
        employeeData.createEmployee(employee);
    }

    public void updateEmployee(Employee employee) {
        employeeData.updateEmployee(employee);
    }

    public void deleteEmployee(int id) {
        employeeData.deleteEmployee(id);
    }
}

// Client code
public class IntegrationExample {
    public static void main(String[] args) {

        // create adapters for CSV and JSON implementation
        EmployeeData csvEmployeeData = new CSVEmployeeDataAdapter();
        EmployeeData jsonEmployeeData = new JSONEmployeeDataAdapter()
            ;

        // use bridge to interact with CSV implementation
        EmployeeManager payrollManager = new EmployeeManager(
            csvEmployeeData);
        payrollManager.createEmployee(new Employee(123, "John Doe"));

        // use bridge to interact with JSON implementation
        EmployeeManager hrManager = new EmployeeManager(
            jsonEmployeeData);
```

```
        Employee employee = hrManager.getEmployeeById(123);
        employee.setSalary(50000);
        hrManager.updateEmployee(employee);
    }
}
```

In summary, using the Bridge pattern with the Adapter pattern can be helpful in solving complex integration problems by allowing us to split a large class or a set of closely related classes into two separate hierarchies and modify the interface of an existing class so that it matches what a client expects.

4.18   Can you provide an example of using the Template Method pattern to support multiple variations of an algorithm with minimal code duplication?

The Template Method pattern is a behavioral design pattern that defines the skeleton of an algorithm in a superclass but lets subclasses override specific steps of the algorithm without changing its structure. This can be useful when you have several subclasses that implement variations of the same algorithm, but most of the algorithm's logic is common to all subclasses. By using the Template Method pattern, you can minimize code duplication and make it easy to add new variations to the algorithm later on.

Here's a simple example that demonstrates how you might use the Template Method pattern to implement a simple sorting algorithm that supports multiple variations:

```
public abstract class SortAlgorithm {
    public final void sort(int[] arr) {
        // Step 1: Perform any pre-processing required
        prepare(arr);

        // Step 2: Perform the actual sorting algorithm (implemented
        //     in a subclass)
        performSort(arr);

        // Step 3: Perform any post-processing required
        cleanup(arr);
    }

    protected void prepare(int[] arr) {
        // Default implementation performs no pre-processing, but can
        //     be overridden by a subclass
    }

    protected abstract void performSort(int[] arr);

    protected void cleanup(int[] arr) {
        // Default implementation performs no post-processing, but can
        //     be overridden by a subclass
    }
}
```

In this example, the 'SortAlgorithm' class defines the skeleton of a sorting algorithm using the Template Method pattern. The 'sort()' method is the Template Method itself, which calls several other methods to carry out the algorithm:

1. 'prepare()' - a hook method that can be overridden by a subclass to perform any pre-processing required before running the sorting algorithm.

2. 'performSort()' - an abstract method that is implemented by a subclass to perform the actual sorting algorithm. This is the only method that must be implemented by a subclass; the others have default implementations that can be overridden if necessary.

3. 'cleanup()' - a hook method that can be overridden by a subclass to perform any post-processing required after the sorting algorithm has run.

Here's an example of a subclass that implements a bubble sort algorithm:

```
public class BubbleSort extends SortAlgorithm {
    @Override
    protected void performSort(int[] arr) {
        for (int i = 0; i < arr.length; i++) {
            for (int j = 1; j < (arr.length - i); j++) {
                if (arr[j - 1] > arr[j]) {
                    // Swap elements
                    int temp = arr[j - 1];
                    arr[j - 1] = arr[j];
                    arr[j] = temp;
                }
            }
        }
    }
}
```

In this example, the 'BubbleSort' class extends the 'SortAlgorithm' class and implements the 'performSort()' method to implement the bubble sort algorithm. The 'prepare()' and 'cleanup()'
methods are not overridden, so they use the default implementations inherited from the 'SortAlgorithm' class.

Here's an example of how you might use the 'SortAlgorithm'
class to run a bubble sort:

```
int[] arr = {5, 2, 8, 3, 1, 6};
SortAlgorithm sort = new BubbleSort();
sort.sort(arr);
```

In this example, we create an integer array and a 'BubbleSort'
object, and then call the 'sort()' method on the 'BubbleSort' object to run the sorting algorithm. Because the 'sort()' method is
defined in the superclass ('SortAlgorithm'), we can easily swap
out different sorting algorithms (such as quicksort or merge
sort) simply by creating a different subclass that overrides the
'performSort()' method. And because the other methods ('pre-
pare()' and 'cleanup()') are hook methods with default implementations, we only need to override them if we need to perform

any additional pre- or post-processing specific to the algorithm
we're using.

4.19   Discuss how using the Abstract Factory pattern can impact the maintainability and scalability of a system when dealing with an evolving product family.

Abstract Factory is a creational design pattern that provides
an interface for creating families of related or dependent objects
without specifying their concrete classes. It allows a client code
to work with abstract interfaces instead of the concrete ones.

In the context of an evolving product family, the Abstract Factory pattern can have a significant impact on the maintainability and scalability of a system. Let's see how:

Maintainability

As the product family evolves over time, new products get
added, and existing products might get updated or removed.
In such cases, the Abstract Factory pattern can make it much
easier to maintain the codebase.

The clients of the abstract factory interface will remain unaffected by the changes made to the concrete implementations of
the products, which makes it easy to incorporate new products
into the existing system without modifying the client code.

Additionally, if a bug is found in one of the concrete product classes, it can be fixed without affecting the rest of the system. This reduces the likelihood of introducing new bugs while fixing the old ones.

In summary, by encapsulating the creation of related objects, the Abstract Factory pattern can make it easier to maintain the system by minimizing the impact of changes to the product family.

Scalability

When dealing with a large product family, the number of concrete classes can grow very quickly. This can lead to a combinatorial explosion of factory methods and client code that is hard to manage.

The Abstract Factory pattern can help with scalability by providing a single interface for creating related objects. This way, the number of classes and methods exposed to the client remains constant, regardless of the size of the product family.

Moreover, if the product family is split into subfamilies, each with its own abstract factory, the scalability of the system can be further improved. It allows new subfamilies to be added independently of the existing ones, reducing the impact of changes across the entire system.

Java Code Examples

Here's a Java code example of the Abstract Factory Pattern:

```java
public interface GUIFactory {
    Button createButton();
    TextField createTextField();
}

public class WinFactory implements GUIFactory {
```

```java
    public Button createButton() {
        return new WinButton();
    }

    public TextField createTextField() {
        return new WinTextField();
    }
}

public class MacFactory implements GUIFactory {
    public Button createButton() {
        return new MacButton();
    }

    public TextField createTextField() {
        return new MacTextField();
    }
}

public interface Button {
    void paint();
}

public class WinButton implements Button {
    public void paint() {
        System.out.println("Rendering Windows button...");
    }
}

public class MacButton implements Button {
    public void paint() {
        System.out.println("Rendering Mac button...");
    }
}

public interface TextField {
    void paint();
}

public class WinTextField implements TextField {
    public void paint() {
        System.out.println("Rendering Windows text field...");
    }
}

public class MacTextField implements TextField {
    public void paint() {
        System.out.println("Rendering Mac text field...");
    }
}

public class Application {
    private GUIFactory factory;
    private Button button;
```

```
        private TextField textField;

        public Application(GUIFactory factory) {
            this.factory = factory;
            button = factory.createButton();
            textField = factory.createTextField();
        }

        public void render() {
            button.paint();
            textField.paint();
        }
    }

    public class Client {
        public static void main(String[] args) {
            GUIFactory factory = null;
            String os = System.getProperty("os.name");
            if (os.toLowerCase().contains("win")) {
                factory = new WinFactory();
            } else {
                factory = new MacFactory();
            }

            Application app = new Application(factory);
            app.render();
        }
    }
```

In this example, the 'GUIFactory' interface is an abstract factory that defines two methods for creating related products:
'createButton()' and 'createTextField()'. Concrete implementations of the 'GUIFactory' interface (i.e., 'WinFactory' and
'MacFactory') create products that are specific to their respective operating systems.

The 'Button' and 'TextField' interfaces define the abstract products that can be created by the abstract factory. Concrete
implementations of these interfaces ('WinButton', 'MacBut-
ton', 'WinTextField', and 'MacTextField') provide operating-
system-specific functionality for rendering buttons and text fields.

Finally, the 'Application' and 'Client' classes demonstrate how
the abstract factory can be used to create operating-system-

specific user interfaces based on the current system. The 'Client'
class reads the current operating system from the system properties and instantiates the appropriate 'GUIFactory', which is
then passed to the 'Application' constructor.

When the 'Application' is instantiated, it creates a 'Button' and
a 'TextField' by calling the appropriate factory methods. The
'render' method then calls the 'paint' methods on each product
to render the user interface on the operating-system-specific
platform.

4.20   How can you apply the Visitor pat-tern to a large object hierarchy with frequent additions of new element types while maintaining the Open/Closed Principle?

The Visitor pattern can be used to traverse a complex object
hierarchy and perform operations on its elements without modifying their classes. However, one challenge with this pattern
is that it requires modifying the Visitor interface every time
a new element type is added to the hierarchy. This violates
the Open/Closed Principle, which states that classes should be
open for extension but closed for modification.

To apply the Visitor pattern while maintaining the Open/-
Closed Principle, we can use the Double Dispatch technique.
This technique involves creating a separate method for each
combination of element type and operation in both the Visitor
interface and the Element hierarchy. This allows new element

types and operations to be added without modifying any existing code.

Consider the following example where we have a complex object
hierarchy that represents mathematical expressions:

```
abstract class Expression {
    abstract double evaluate();
}

class Number extends Expression {
    double value;
    double evaluate() { return value; }
}

class BinaryOperation extends Expression {
    char operator;
    Expression left;
    Expression right;
    double evaluate() { ... }
}
```

Suppose we want to implement a 'Printer' Visitor that prints
out the expression in a human-readable format. Without Double Dispatch, we would need to modify the Visitor interface
every time a new type of Expression is added:

```
interface Printer {
    void printNumber(Number number);
    void printBinaryOperation(BinaryOperation binaryOperation);
    // need to add new method for each new type of Expression
}
```

With Double Dispatch, we add a method for each combination
of Expression type and Visitor operation in both the Visitor
interface and the Element hierarchy:

```
interface Expression {
    void accept(Printer printer);
}

class Number implements Expression {
    double value;
    void accept(Printer printer) {
        printer.visitNumber(this);
```

```
    }
}

class BinaryOperation implements Expression {
    char operator;
    Expression left;
    Expression right;
    void accept(Printer printer) {
        printer.visitBinaryOperation(this);
    }
}

interface Printer {
    void visitNumber(Number number);
    void visitBinaryOperation(BinaryOperation binaryOperation);
}

class SimplePrinter implements Printer {
    void visitNumber(Number number) {
        System.out.print(number.value);
    }
    void visitBinaryOperation(BinaryOperation binaryOperation) {
        System.out.print("(");
        binaryOperation.left.accept(this);
        System.out.print("␣" + binaryOperation.operator + "␣");
        binaryOperation.right.accept(this);
        System.out.print(")");
    }
}
```

Now we can add new types of Expressions without modifying
the Visitor interface or any existing code:

```
class UnaryOperation implements Expression {
    char operator;
    Expression expression;
    void accept(Printer printer) {
        printer.visitUnaryOperation(this);
    }
}

interface Printer {
    void visitNumber(Number number);
    void visitBinaryOperation(BinaryOperation binaryOperation);
    void visitUnaryOperation(UnaryOperation unaryOperation);
}

class SimplePrinter implements Printer {
    void visitNumber(Number number) {
        System.out.print(number.value);
    }
```

```
    void visitBinaryOperation(BinaryOperation binaryOperation) {
        System.out.print("(");
        binaryOperation.left.accept(this);
        System.out.print(" " + binaryOperation.operator + " ");
        binaryOperation.right.accept(this);
        System.out.print(")");
    }
    void visitUnaryOperation(UnaryOperation unaryOperation) {
        System.out.print("(" + unaryOperation.operator);
        unaryOperation.expression.accept(this);
        System.out.print(")");
    }
}
```

In summary, Double Dispatch allows us to apply the Visitor pattern to a large and evolving object hierarchy while maintaining the Open/Closed Principle by adding a method for each combination of Element type and Visitor operation in both the Visitor interface and the Element hierarchy.

Chapter 5

Expert

5.1 Discuss how the Singleton pattern can impact testability and maintainability in a system, and propose alternative patterns to address these concerns.

Singleton pattern is one of the most frequently used design patterns in software development. It is a creational pattern that ensures that only one instance of a class can be created, and provides a global point of access to that instance. While Singleton pattern may seem useful in some use cases, it often creates several issues, especially with respect to testability and maintainability.

Impact on Testability:

The Singleton pattern can make testing difficult for several reasons:

1. **Dependencies:** Singleton classes are usually tightly coupled to other classes in the system. If a class is tightly coupled, it can be difficult to test it in isolation without the other dependencies. Thus, when writing tests for a class that depends on a Singleton, one may need to mock out the entire Singleton and its dependencies in order to test it properly.

2. **Global state:** Singleton classes introduce global state into the system. Global state is hard to isolate and control, making it harder to test. Since a Singleton instance is global, any state changes made to it during one test will affect the execution of the subsequent tests.

3. **Constructor issues:** The constructor of a Singleton class is private or protected, which makes it difficult or impossible to instantiate a new instance of the class for testing purposes.

Impact on Maintainability:

The Singleton pattern can also impact maintainability of a system. Some issues include:

1. **Lack of flexibility:** The Singleton pattern creates a rigid structure whereby only one instance of the class can exist. If the design of the system changes and there is a need for more than one instance of the class, it can be difficult to modify the implementation.

2. **Singletons are difficult to replace:** Since the Singleton is often hard-coded into the implementation of a system, it can be difficult to replace it with another implementation, as this would require changing code throughout the system that

depends on it.

3. **Concurrency issues:** When multiple threads access a Singleton object simultaneously, it can cause problems with synchronization and introduce concurrency issues.

Given these issues, there are several alternatives to the Singleton pattern that can address these concerns:

1. **Dependency injection:** Dependency injection is a technique whereby dependencies (including Singletons) are passed to a class as constructor arguments. This makes it easier to test classes in isolation, since it is possible to pass in mock objects for testing.

2. **Factory pattern:** Instead of using a Singleton to create objects, a factory pattern can be used to create objects and manage their lifecycle. This pattern can encapsulate the creation of objects and reduce coupling between classes.

3. **ThreadLocal pattern:** If a Singleton is needed for thread-specific data, a ThreadLocal pattern can be used instead. This pattern provides a separate instance of a class for each thread and avoids concurrency issues.

Here is an example of using the factory pattern in Java to create objects and manage their lifecycle:

```
public interface MyInterface {
  // methods
}

public class MyFactory {
  private Map<String, MyInterface> instances = new HashMap<>();

  public MyInterface getInstance(String key) {
    if (!instances.containsKey(key)) {
      instances.put(key, createInstance(key));
    }
```

```
    return instances.get(key);
  }

  private MyInterface createInstance(String key) {
    // create an instance of MyInterface based on the key
  }
}

public class MyClass {
  private MyInterface instance;

  public MyClass(MyFactory factory, String key) {
    this.instance = factory.getInstance(key);
  }

  // use instance as needed
}
```

In this example, each instance of MyClass uses a MyInterface
implementation that is created through a factory. The implementation of the factory can be modified as needed, and the
dependency on the factory can be easily mock in unit tests.

5.2   Describe how the Abstract Factory pattern can be used in a plug-in architecture to support extensibility and flexibility of a system.

The Abstract Factory pattern is a creational design pattern
that provides an interface for creating families of related or
dependent objects without specifying their concrete classes. In
this pattern, a client uses an abstract factory to create a family
of related objects, and the concrete factories then create the
concrete objects. This allows for the creation of families of
objects that can be interchanged easily, without impacting the
external code.

A plug-in architecture is a software architecture that allows for the extension of a software system via the use of plugins or modules that add functionality to the system. Plug-ins can be created by third-party developers and add new features or functionality to the core system without changing the core code.

The Abstract Factory pattern can be used in a plug-in architecture to provide a flexible and extensible system. Each plugin can provide its own concrete factory that encapsulates the creation of its objects, which can be thought of as a specific family of related objects. The core system can then use the abstract factory interfaces to create the objects from the plugins, without needing to know which concrete factory is being used.

For example, consider a system that needs to provide support for different types of databases. A plugin architecture can be used to allow third-party developers to create new database plugins that the system can use to connect to different types of databases. An Abstract Factory pattern can be used to create abstract factory interfaces that define how the system should create database connections, queries, and other related objects. The concrete factories for each plugin can then implement these interfaces to create their specific database objects, such as a MySQLConnectionFactory or a PostgreSQLConnectionFactory. The core system can use the abstract factory interfaces to create the required objects, without knowing which concrete factory is being used. This allows for the system to be easily extended with new plugins that provide support for new types of databases.

Here's an example Java code for the Abstract Factory pattern in a plug-in architecture:

```
// Abstract Factory interface
public interface DatabaseConnectionFactory {
```

```
    public DatabaseConnection createConnection();
}

// Concrete factory for MySQL
public class MySQLConnectionFactory implements
    DatabaseConnectionFactory {
    public DatabaseConnection createConnection() {
        // create a new MySQL connection
    }
}

// Concrete factory for PostgreSQL
public class PostgreSQLConnectionFactory implements
    DatabaseConnectionFactory {
    public DatabaseConnection createConnection() {
        // create a new PostgreSQL connection
    }
}

// Plugin interface
public interface DatabasePlugin {
    public DatabaseConnectionFactory createConnectionFactory();
}

// Concrete plugin for MySQL
public class MySQLDatabasePlugin implements DatabasePlugin {
    public DatabaseConnectionFactory createConnectionFactory() {
        return new MySQLConnectionFactory();
    }
}

// Concrete plugin for PostgreSQL
public class PostgreSQLDatabasePlugin implements DatabasePlugin {
    public DatabaseConnectionFactory createConnectionFactory() {
        return new PostgreSQLConnectionFactory();
    }
}

// Core system
public class DatabaseSystem {
    private DatabaseConnectionFactory factory;

    public DatabaseSystem(DatabaseConnectionFactory factory) {
        this.factory = factory;
    }

    public DatabaseConnection getConnection() {
        return factory.createConnection();
    }
}

// Example usage
DatabasePlugin mysqlPlugin = new MySQLDatabasePlugin();
DatabasePlugin postgresPlugin = new PostgreSQLDatabasePlugin();
```

```
DatabaseConnectionFactory mysqlFactory = mysqlPlugin.
    createConnectionFactory();
DatabaseConnectionFactory postgresFactory = postgresPlugin.
    createConnectionFactory();

DatabaseSystem mysqlSystem = new DatabaseSystem(mysqlFactory);
DatabaseSystem postgresSystem = new DatabaseSystem(postgresFactory);

DatabaseConnection mysqlConnection = mysqlSystem.getConnection();
DatabaseConnection postgresConnection = postgresSystem.getConnection
    ();
```

In this example, the abstract factory interface 'DatabaseConnectionFactory' defines the contract for creating a database connection. The concrete factories 'MySQLConnectionFactory' and 'PostgreSQLConnectionFactory' implement the interface for specific types of databases. The plugins 'MySQLDatabasePlugin' and 'PostgreSQLDatabasePlugin' provide the concrete factories for each type of database. Finally, the 'DatabaseSystem' class uses the abstract factory interface to create the required objects, without knowing which concrete factory is being used.

5.3   Explain how the Observer pattern can be implemented with reactive programming concepts like Observables and Subscribers.

The Observer pattern is a design pattern that allows objects to subscribe to and receive notifications of changes to a specific subject, which is often called an observable or publisher. The reactive programming paradigm involves working with streams of data that can be observed and manipulated to produce reactive behavior. In this context, the Observer pattern can be implemented using Observables and Subscribers.

Observables in reactive programming represent a stream of data that can be observed. They emit values over time and notify any subscribed Subscriber objects whenever a new value is emitted. Subscribers are the objects that observe the Observable and react to the emitted values.

To implement the Observer pattern using Observables and Subscribers, the following steps can be taken:

1. Define the Observable: The first step is to define the observable that will emit values over time. This can be done using a variety of methods, including creating an Observable from scratch or transforming an existing one.

Example of creating an Observable using the fromIterable method in RxJava:

```
Observable<String> observable = Observable.fromIterable(Arrays.
    asList("Item 1", "Item 2", "Item 3"));
```

2. Subscribe to the Observable: Once the Observable is defined, a Subscriber object can subscribe to it. This can be done using the subscribe method, which takes in a lambda function that specifies the actions to be taken when a new value is emitted by the Observable.

Example of subscribing to the Observable using lambda expressions in RxJava:

```
observable.subscribe(
    item -> System.out.println(item), //onNext action
    error -> System.err.println(error), //onError action
    () -> System.out.println("Done") //onComplete action
);
```

3. Emit values from the Observable: The Observable can now emit values over time. Each time a value is emitted, the Subscriber will receive a notification and execute the specified actions.

Example of emitting values from the Observable in RxJava:

```
observable.subscribe(
    item -> System.out.println(item), //onNext action
    error -> System.err.println(error), //onError action
    () -> System.out.println("Done") //onComplete action
);
```

In conclusion, the Observer pattern can be implemented using Observables and Subscribers in reactive programming. Observables emit values over time and notify any subscribed Subscribers whenever a new value is emitted, allowing objects to subscribe to and receive notifications of changes to a specific subject.

5.4   How would you handle the Decorator pattern with multiple decorators that need to be applied in a specific order, and how would you handle potential conflicts?

The Decorator pattern provides a flexible alternative to inheritance for extending the functionality of a class at runtime. However, when we have multiple decorators in use, we may need to apply them in a specific order to achieve the desired behavior.

To handle multiple decorators in a specific order, we can chain

them together in a particular sequence. Each decorator wraps
the component it decorates, and the wrapped component is
passed along the chain until it reaches the final decorator in the
sequence. In this way, each decorator adds its own behavior to
the component and passes the modified component to the next
decorator in the chain until the final behavior is achieved.

To illustrate this, let's consider an example of a coffee shop
application that allows customers to order different types of
coffee with extra toppings. We can have multiple decorators
that add different toppings, such as milk, sugar, whipped cream,
and cinnamon.

We can start by defining an interface representing the basic
coffee component:

```
public interface Coffee {
    double getCost();
    String getDescription();
}
```

Next, we can create a concrete implementation of the coffee
component:

```
public class SimpleCoffee implements Coffee {
    @Override
    public double getCost() {
        return 1.0;
    }

    @Override
    public String getDescription() {
        return "Simple coffee";
    }
}
```

Now, we can define the decorator interface, which extends the
Coffee interface and adds the functionality of adding extra toppings:

```
public interface CoffeeDecorator extends Coffee {
}
```

We can implement the decorator interface for each topping we want to add, such as milk, sugar, whipped cream, and cinnamon. Each decorator adds the cost and description of its topping to the wrapped coffee component:

```
public class MilkDecorator implements CoffeeDecorator {
    private Coffee coffee;

    public MilkDecorator(Coffee coffee) {
        this.coffee = coffee;
    }

    @Override
    public double getCost() {
        return coffee.getCost() + 0.5;
    }

    @Override
    public String getDescription() {
        return coffee.getDescription() + ", milk";
    }
}

public class SugarDecorator implements CoffeeDecorator {
    private Coffee coffee;

    public SugarDecorator(Coffee coffee) {
        this.coffee = coffee;
    }

    @Override
    public double getCost() {
        return coffee.getCost() + 0.2;
    }

    @Override
    public String getDescription() {
        return coffee.getDescription() + ", sugar";
    }
}

// Similar decorators for whipped cream and cinnamon
```

Finally, we can use the decorators in a specific order to create a custom coffee with the desired toppings:

```
Coffee customCoffee = new SugarDecorator(new WhippedCreamDecorator(
                    new MilkDecorator(new SimpleCoffee())));
System.out.println(customCoffee.getDescription() + " costs $" +
    customCoffee.getCost());
```

In this example, we apply the decorators in the order of Milk, WhippedCream, Sugar, and SimpleCoffee. The output of the code will be:

```
Simple coffee, milk, whipped cream, sugar costs $2.2
```

In case of potential conflicts, we need to carefully design our decorators to avoid overriding each other's functionality. For example, we can have a decorator that adds more coffee instead of water, and this decorator should be applied before any decorator that adds milk, to avoid diluting the coffee flavor. In general, we should follow the Single Responsibility Principle and design our decorators to add independent and cohesive features to the component they decorate.

5.5   Discuss the benefits and drawbacks of using the Strategy pattern with a context object versus using dependency injection or inversion of control containers.

The Strategy pattern is a commonly used pattern in software design that allows for a dynamic selection of an algorithm at runtime. There are two main approaches to implement the Strategy pattern: using a context object or using dependency injection (DI) or inversion of control (IoC) containers. Both approaches have their benefits and drawbacks.

Using a Context Object

In this approach, the context object contains a reference to an instance of a concrete strategy object. The context object delegates a major part of its functionality to the strategy object.

Benefits:

1. **Increased Flexibility**: The context object can change its behavior dynamically by selecting a different strategy object. This is particularly useful when a system needs to support various alternatives for different operations.

2. **Cleaner Code**: The Strategy pattern with a context object can provide cleaner code by encapsulating each algorithm implementation separately, making the code base more modular.

Drawbacks:

1. **Complexity:** The context object needs to have knowledge of all the available strategies, and this can result in a complex and cluttered design.

2. **Lack of Extensibility**: The context object can be hard to extend when new strategies need to be added.

Using Dependency Injection or Inversion of Control Containers

The DI and IoC containers work by registering dependencies at runtime instead of during compile time. With the Strategy pattern, you can use DI or IoC containers to inject the instance of the concrete strategy object.

Benefits:

1. **Improved Code Maintainability**: By using DI and IoC containers, the code is more modular and easier to maintain. It also helps eliminate code duplication and helps manage dependencies efficiently.

2. **Simplifies Design**: Using the DI and IoC approach can also simplify the design and remove the need for a context object.

Drawbacks:

1. **Learning Curve**: adoption of DI and IoC containers can be challenging to understand for developers who are just starting and can result in a steep learning curve.

2. **Performance Overhead**: Injecting dependencies via IoC containers can come with a performance overhead, and this can impact application performance.

Example:

Using the DI and IoC approach, one popular library in Java that can be useful in this scenario is Spring Framework. The code below demonstrates the use of Spring Framework to inject different implementations of the Strategy interface into a service object.

```
public interface Strategy {
    void algorithm ();
}

@Component
@Qualifier("strategy1")
public class StrategyImpl1 implements Strategy {
    public void algorithm() {
        // implementation
    }
```

```
}
@Component
@Qualifier("strategy2")
public class StrategyImpl2 implements Strategy {
  public void algorithm() {
    // implementation
  }
}

@Service
public class Service {
  private final Strategy strategy;

  public Service(@Qualifier("strategy1") Strategy strategy) {
    this.strategy = strategy;
  }

  public void perform() {
    strategy.algorithm();
  }
}
```

In the example above, we use the Spring Framework to inject
two different implementations of the Strategy interface into the
Service object. The @Qualifier annotation helps select the implementation to inject based on a defined name. This is one way
to achieve the Strategy pattern using DI or IoC containers.

In conclusion, both approaches to implementing the Strategy
pattern have benefits and drawbacks, and the choice depends
on the requirements and characteristics of the system. The context object approach offers more flexibility, while the DI and
IoC approach provide simpler code design and better maintainability. A well-designed system will use a combination of both
approaches to maximize the benefits and minimize the drawbacks.

5.6   Explain how the State pattern can be combined with other behavioral patterns like the Mediator or Command patterns to manage complex systems.

The State pattern is a behavioral software design pattern that allows an object to behave differently based on its internal state. The Mediator pattern is also a behavioral pattern that helps to centralize communication between multiple objects. The Command pattern, on the other hand, is used to encapsulate a request as an object, allowing it to be treated as a standalone entity.

The State pattern can be combined with other patterns like Mediator or Command to manage complex systems because it helps to simplify the system and manage dependencies between objects. For example, a complex system might have multiple objects with different states, and it might be difficult to manage the transitions between these states. By using the State pattern, we can encapsulate the state-specific behavior into separate objects, and use a context object to manage the state transitions.

Now let's see how the State pattern can be combined with other patterns:

1) State pattern + Mediator pattern: In this combination, the Mediator pattern can act as a central hub, managing the communication between objects that have different states. For instance, consider a vending machine that has multiple objects such as a coin, candy dispenser, and display. By using the Mediator pattern, we can simplify the system, and by using the

State pattern, we can manage the state transitions of the objects. The Mediator object can keep track of the current state of the vending machine and route the requests to the appropriate object based on its current state.

Here's an example of this combination with Java code:

```
interface VendingMachineState {
    void insertCoin(int amount);
    void selectProduct(String code);
    void dispenseProduct();
}

class NoCoinState implements VendingMachineState {
    private final VendingMachine vendingMachine;
    public NoCoinState(VendingMachine vm) { this.vendingMachine = vm
        ;}
    public void insertCoin(int amount) {
        vendingMachine.setCurrentState(vendingMachine.
            coinInsertedState);
        vendingMachine.addBalance(amount);
    }
    public void selectProduct(String code) {
        System.out.println("Please insert a coin first!");
    }
    public void dispenseProduct() {
        System.out.println("Please insert a coin first!");
    }
}

class CoinInsertedState implements VendingMachineState {
    private final VendingMachine vendingMachine;
    public CoinInsertedState(VendingMachine vm) { this.
        vendingMachine = vm;}
    public void insertCoin(int amount) {
        vendingMachine.addBalance(amount);
    }
    public void selectProduct(String code) {
        if(vendingMachine.getProduct(code) != null){
            vendingMachine.setCurrentState(vendingMachine.
                productSelectedState);
            vendingMachine.setSelectedProductCode(code);
        }else{
            System.out.println("Invalid product code!");
        }
    }
    public void dispenseProduct() {
        System.out.println("Please select a product first!");
    }
}
```

```java
class ProductSelectedState implements VendingMachineState {
    private final VendingMachine vendingMachine;
    public ProductSelectedState(VendingMachine vm) { this.
        vendingMachine = vm;}
    public void insertCoin(int amount) {
        vendingMachine.addBalance(amount);
    }
    public void selectProduct(String code) {
        System.out.println("Please wait, dispensing product!");
    }
    public void dispenseProduct() {
        vendingMachine.dispenseSelectedProduct();
        vendingMachine.setCurrentState(vendingMachine.noCoinState);
    }
}

class VendingMachine {
    VendingMachineState noCoinState;
    VendingMachineState coinInsertedState;
    VendingMachineState productSelectedState;
    VendingMachineState currentState;
    int balance = 0;
    String selectedProductCode;
    Map<String, Integer> inventory = new HashMap<>();
    Map<String, Integer> prices = new HashMap<>();

    public VendingMachine() {
        noCoinState = new NoCoinState(this);
        coinInsertedState = new CoinInsertedState(this);
        productSelectedState = new ProductSelectedState(this);
        setCurrentState(noCoinState);
    }

    public void setCurrentState(VendingMachineState state) {
        this.currentState = state;
    }

    public void addBalance(int amount) {
        this.balance += amount;
        System.out.println("Balance added: " + amount);
    }

    public void dispenseSelectedProduct() {
        int price = prices.get(selectedProductCode);
        inventory.put(selectedProductCode, inventory.get(
            selectedProductCode) - 1);
        System.out.println("Product Dispensed: " +
            selectedProductCode);
        System.out.println("Balance returned: " + (balance - price));
        balance = 0;
    }

    public void selectProduct(String code) {
        currentState.selectProduct(code);
```

```
    }

    public void insertCoin(int amount) {
        currentState.insertCoin(amount);
    }

    public void dispenseProduct() {
        currentState.dispenseProduct();
    }

    public void addProduct(String code, int count, int price) {
        inventory.put(code, count);
        prices.put(code, price);
    }

    public int getProduct(String code) {
        if (inventory.get(code) > 0) {
            return prices.get(code);
        } else {
            return 0;
        }
    }

}
```

In this code, we have implemented a Vending Machine using the State pattern. We have three states i.e NoCoinState, CoinInsertedState, ProductSelectedState. We also have defined the Mediator class VendingMachine, that manages the communication between different objects i.e coin dispenser, product dispenser, etc. We can see that the Mediator manages the state transitions of objects by calling their corresponding methods based on the current state.

2) State pattern + Command pattern: In this combination, we can use the Command pattern to encapsulate a state transition as an object. For instance, consider a door with multiple states, and we want to create a log of every state transition. By using the State pattern, we can define each state as an object, and by using the Command pattern, we can encapsulate the state transitions as Command objects.

Here's an example of this combination with Java code:

```java
interface DoorState {
    void open();
    void close();
    String getName();
}

class OpenState implements DoorState {
    private final Door door;
    OpenState(Door door) { this.door = door; }
    public void open() {
        System.out.println("Door is already open!");
    }
    public void close() {
        door.setCurrentState(door.getCloseState());
        System.out.println("Door is closed!");
    }
    public String getName() {
        return "Open";
    }
}

class CloseState implements DoorState {
    private final Door door;
    CloseState(Door door) { this.door = door; }
    public void open() {
        door.setCurrentState(door.getOpenState());
        System.out.println("Door is open!");
    }
    public void close() {
        System.out.println("Door is already closed!");
    }
    public String getName() {
        return "Close";
    }
}

class Door {
    private DoorState openState = new OpenState(this);
    private DoorState closeState = new CloseState(this);
    private DoorState currentState = closeState;
    private List<DoorCommand> commands = new ArrayList<>();
    public void setCurrentState(DoorState state) {
        currentState = state;
    }
    public void open() {
        commands.add(new DoorOpenCommand(currentState));
        currentState.open();
    }
    public void close() {
        commands.add(new DoorCloseCommand(currentState));
        currentState.close();
```

```
    }
    public DoorState getOpenState() {
        return openState;
    }
    public DoorState getCloseState() {
        return closeState;
    }
    public void printCommands(){
        System.out.println("List of commands executed:");
        for (DoorCommand command : commands) {
            System.out.println(command.getName());
        }
    }
}

interface DoorCommand {
    void execute();
    String getName();
}

class DoorOpenCommand implements DoorCommand {
    private final DoorState state;
    DoorOpenCommand(DoorState state) { this.state = state; }
    public void execute() {
        state.open();
    }
    public String getName() {
        return state.getName() + " command executed: Door is open.";
    }
}

class DoorCloseCommand implements DoorCommand {
    private final DoorState state;
    DoorCloseCommand(DoorState state) { this.state = state; }
    public void execute() {
        state.close();
    }
    public String getName() {
        return state.getName() + " command executed: Door is closed."
            ;
    }
}
```

In this code, we have implemented a Door and defined its two states i.e OpenState and CloseState using the State pattern. We have also defined the Command pattern, which encapsulates the state transitions as Command objects. We maintain the list of executed commands using the list of DoorCommand objects.

In conclusion, we can say that the State pattern is a powerful tool for managing complex systems, and by combining it with other behavioral patterns such as Mediator or Command, we can further simplify the system and make it more manageable.

5.7   Describe the challenges and potential solutions when implementing the Adapter pattern in a system with multiple adapter layers or cascading adapters.

The Adapter pattern is commonly used in software development to enable communication between incompatible interfaces or systems. However, in systems with multiple adapter layers or cascading adapters, implementing the Adapter pattern can create a complex architecture with potential challenges.

One challenge of implementing multiple adapter layers is the risk of creating a tightly coupled system. Each adapter layer depends on the layer beneath it, and any changes made to a lower layer can have a ripple effect on the entire system. This can lead to maintenance and scalability issues in the long term.

Another challenge is defining the responsibility of each adapter layer. With multiple layers, it can be difficult to determine which layer is responsible for a particular function or behavior. This can lead to confusion and make it challenging to debug issues when they arise.

However, there are potential solutions to these challenges when implementing the Adapter pattern in a system with multiple adapter layers.

One is to use the Dependency Inversion Principle (DIP) to reduce coupling between adapter layers. This principle suggests that higher-level modules should not depend on lower-level modules directly but rather on abstractions. Using abstractions as a middle layer between adapters can decouple the system and make it easier to modify or replace any of the adapters without affecting the others.

Another solution is to define each adapter layer's responsibility clearly. This can be done by using an interface to define the expected behavior of each adapter layer. By defining an interface, the contract between the layers is clear, and each adapter layer can be tested individually.

Java Code Example:

```java
// Example of adapter pattern with two adapter layers

// Interface for the expected behavior of adapter layer 1
interface AdapterLayer1 {
    public void method1();
}

// Concrete implementation of adapter layer 1
class ConcreteAdapterLayer1 implements AdapterLayer1 {
    public void method1() {
        // implementation
    }
}

// Interface for the expected behavior of adapter layer 2
interface AdapterLayer2 {
    public void method2();
}

// Concrete implementation of adapter layer 2
class ConcreteAdapterLayer2 implements AdapterLayer2 {
    private AdapterLayer1 adapterLayer1;

    // Constructor injection of adapter layer 1
    public ConcreteAdapterLayer2(AdapterLayer1 adapterLayer1) {
        this.adapterLayer1 = adapterLayer1;
    }

    public void method2() {
```

```
    // implementation that uses adapter layer 1
    adapterLayer1.method1();
  }
}

// Usage example
AdapterLayer1 adapter1 = new ConcreteAdapterLayer1();
AdapterLayer2 adapter2 = new ConcreteAdapterLayer2(adapter1);
adapter2.method2();
```

In the code example above, we have two adapter layers. Adapter
layer 2 depends on adapter layer 1 to perform its tasks. To
avoid creating a tightly coupled system, we utilize constructor
injection to provide adapter layer 1 to adapter layer 2. We
also define interfaces for each adapter layer, which makes the
responsibilities of each layer clear.

5.8   Discuss how the Command pattern can be used in conjunction with the CQRS (Command Query Responsibility Segregation) pattern in distributed systems.

The Command pattern and the CQRS pattern are two design
patterns that can be used together in distributed systems to
provide a more robust and scalable architecture. In this section, we will discuss how the Command pattern can be used in
conjunction with the CQRS pattern.

The Command pattern is a behavioral design pattern that encapsulates a request as an object, thereby letting us parameterize clients with different requests, queue or log requests, and
support undoable operations. It has four primary components:

1. Command: The object encapsulating a request.

2. Receiver: The object that operates on a request.

3. Invoker: The object that requests the command to execute the request.

4. Client: The object that sets the concrete command to execute the request.

The CQRS pattern is an architectural pattern that separates the read and write operations of an application's data model into separate components. It has two primary components:

1. Command: The object that represents a write operation (add, update, delete, etc.).

2. Query: The object that represents a read operation (retrieve data).

CQRS has become a popular pattern in distributed systems to improve scalability, performance, and responsiveness. In CQRS, the write operation (Command) and the read operation (Query) are kept separate. This enables us to use different storage (e.g., SQL databases for write and NoSQL databases for read). It also allows us to have different scaling strategies for read and write operations.

Now, let's see how the Command pattern can be used in conjunction with the CQRS pattern.

1. Command Handler: In the CQRS pattern, we have a Command object that represents a write operation. We can use the Command pattern to encapsulate this Command object as a separate object, which we call Command Handler. The Command Handler processes the Command object by calling the Receiver object.

2. Invoker: In the Command pattern, we have an Invoker object that requests the command to execute the request. In the context of CQRS, the Invoker object can be the Application Service layer that receives the Command object and requests the Command Handler to process the Command object.

3. Receiver: The Receiver object in the Command pattern is the object that operates on a request. In the context of CQRS, the Receiver object can be the Aggregate Root that encapsulates the business logic for a particular domain entity. The Command Handler calls the Aggregate Root to process the Command object.

4. Client: In the Command pattern, the Client object sets the concrete Command to execute the request. In the context of CQRS, the Client object can be any component that generates the Command object, such as the User Interface layer or Messaging layer.

Here is an example Java implementation of the Command pattern and CQRS pattern:

```java
// Command Interface
public interface Command {
    void execute();
}

// Concrete Command
public class AddProductCommand implements Command {
    private final String productId;
    private final String name;
    private final BigDecimal price;
    private final int quantity;

    public AddProductCommand(String productId, String name,
        BigDecimal price, int quantity) {
        this.productId = productId;
        this.name = name;
        this.price = price;
        this.quantity = quantity;
    }

    @Override
```

```
    public void execute() {
        // Call the Command Handler
        ApplicationService.addProduct(this);
    }

    // Getters
}
// Command Handler
public class AddProductCommandHandler {
    public void handle(AddProductCommand command) {
        // Call the Aggregate Root
        ProductAggregate.addProduct(command);
    }
}

// Aggregate Root
public class ProductAggregate {
    public static void addProduct(AddProductCommand command) {
        // Business logic to add a product
    }
}

// Client
public class AddProductClient {
    public void addProduct() {
        // Generate the Command object
        AddProductCommand command = new AddProductCommand(productId,
            name, price, quantity);
        // Set the Concrete Command to execute the request
        command.execute();
    }
}

// Application Service
public class ApplicationService {
    public static void addProduct(AddProductCommand command) {
        // Call the Command Handler to process the Command object
        AddProductCommandHandler handler = new
            AddProductCommandHandler();
        handler.handle(command);
    }
}
```

In this example, we have a Command interface, AddProduct-Command as a Concrete Command, AddProductCommand-Handler as a Command Handler, ProductAggregate as a Receiver, and AddProductClient as a Client that generates the Command object. The ApplicationService acts as an Invoker that requests the Command Handler to process the Command object.

In conclusion, the Command pattern is a suitable pattern to use in conjunction with the CQRS pattern in distributed systems. It helps to encapsulate and process the Command object, while CQRS separates the read and write operations of an application's data model into separate components. Together, they provide a scalable, performant, and responsive architecture.

5.9   Compare the Prototype pattern with the Object Pool pattern in terms of performance, memory usage, and garbage collection implications.

Prototype pattern and Object Pool pattern are two different software design patterns that are used to create and manage objects in an efficient and scalable way. In this answer, we will compare the performance, memory usage, and garbage collection implications of these two patterns.

Prototype Pattern

Prototype pattern is a creational pattern that allows creating new objects by copying existing objects. The prototype pattern involves creating a prototype object and then cloning it to create new objects. The prototype objects are typically created on demand and then cached or stored for future use. This pattern is useful when creating new objects is expensive, and when there is a need to create objects with similar properties.

Performance

The performance of the prototype pattern is generally good, especially when creating a large number of objects with similar properties. The reason for this is that the overhead of creating the prototype object is only incurred once, and subsequent object creation involves cloning the prototype object, which is much faster than creating a new object from scratch.

Memory Usage

Memory usage of prototype pattern is higher than the Object Pool pattern since the prototype objects are stored in memory until they are needed. However, this memory usage is typically not a concern since the number of prototype objects is usually limited.

Garbage Collection

Garbage collection in the prototype pattern is usually not a concern since the prototype objects are typically created once and then cached or stored for future use. This means that there is no need to worry about cleaning up objects that are no longer needed.

Example

```java
public abstract class Shape implements Cloneable {
    private String id;
    protected String type;

    public String getId() {
        return id;
    }

    public void setId(String id) {
        this.id = id;
    }

    public String getType() {
        return type;
```

```
    }

    public abstract void draw();

    public Object clone() {
        Object clone = null;

        try {
            clone = super.clone();

        } catch (CloneNotSupportedException e) {
            e.printStackTrace();
        }

        return clone;
    }
}

public class Circle extends Shape {

    public Circle() {
        type = "Circle";
    }

    @Override
    public void draw() {
        System.out.println("Inside␣Circle::draw()␣method.");
    }
}
```

Object Pool Pattern

Object Pool pattern is a creational pattern that uses a pool of
reusable objects to reduce the overhead of creating new objects.
The Object Pool pattern involves creating a pool of objects
and then reusing them as needed. This pattern is useful when
creating new objects is expensive, and when there is a need to
limit the number of objects that are created.

Performance

The performance of the Object Pool pattern is usually good,
especially when creating a large number of objects with similar
properties. The reason for this is that the overhead of creating the objects is only incurred once when the pool is created,

and subsequent object creation involves reusing existing objects, which is much faster than creating new objects from scratch.

Memory Usage

Memory usage of the Object Pool pattern is lower than the prototype pattern since the objects are reused from the pool instead of creating new objects. This means that the number of objects in memory is limited to the size of the pool.

Garbage Collection

Garbage collection in the Object Pool pattern can be a concern since the pool may contain objects that are no longer needed. In this case, the pool must be periodically cleaned up to remove unused objects from memory.

Example

```
public interface Connection {
    public void execute(String sql);
    public void close();
}

public class MySqlConnection implements Connection {
    private String url;
    private String user;
    private String password;

    public MySqlConnection(String url, String user, String password)
        {
        this.url = url;
        this.user = user;
        this.password = password;
        connect();
    }

    private void connect() {
        // Connect to database
    }

    public void execute(String sql) {
        // Execute SQL
    }
```

```java
    public void close() {
        // Close connection
    }
}
public class ConnectionPool {
    private List<Connection> connections = new ArrayList<Connection
        >();
    private String url;
    private String user;
    private String password;

    public ConnectionPool(String url, String user, String password)
        {
        this.url = url;
        this.user = user;
        this.password = password;

        for (int i = 0; i < 10; i++) {
            connections.add(new MySqlConnection(url, user, password));
        }
    }

    public Connection getConnection() {
        if (connections.isEmpty()) {
            throw new RuntimeException("No connections available");
        }

        return connections.remove(0);
    }

    public void releaseConnection(Connection connection) {
        connections.add(connection);
    }
}
```

Conclusion

Both the Prototype pattern and Object Pool pattern are useful
for creating and managing objects in an efficient and scalable
way. The choice of pattern depends on the specific requirements
of the application, such as the need to limit the number of objects in memory, the frequency of object creation, and the cost
of object creation. While Prototype pattern is useful when creating objects with similar properties, the Object Pool pattern
is useful when there is a need to limit the number of objects
that are created.

5.10   Explain how the Builder pattern can be adapted to handle concurrent object creation in a multi-threaded environment.

The Builder pattern can be used to create complex objects by separating the object creation logic from their representation. This pattern can also be adapted to handle concurrent object creation in a multi-threaded environment by implementing the Builder as follows:

1. Use thread-local storage: Create a Builder instance for each thread and use thread-local storage to store it. This way, each thread can have its own instance of the Builder and can use it independently to create objects without interfering with other threads.

2. Synchronize the build method: To ensure that only one thread can build an object at a time, the build method can be synchronized. This way, if multiple threads attempt to build objects simultaneously, only one thread will be allowed to build the object while the others wait.

3. Use immutable objects: The objects created by the Builder pattern should preferably be immutable, i.e., their internal state should not change after creation. This makes them safe to use in a multi-threaded environment without any additional synchronization.

Here is an example implementation of the Builder pattern adapted for concurrent object creation in Java:

```
public class ComplexObject {
```

```
    // fields and methods of the complex object
}

public class ComplexObjectBuilder {
    private int field1;
    private String field2;
    // other fields of the builder

    public ComplexObjectBuilder setField1(int field1) {
        this.field1 = field1;
        return this;
    }

    public ComplexObjectBuilder setField2(String field2) {
        this.field2 = field2;
        return this;
    }
    // other setter methods

    public synchronized ComplexObject build() {
        // create and return the complex object
        ComplexObject obj = new ComplexObject(field1, field2, ...);
        return obj;
    }
}

public class ClientThread implements Runnable {
    private ThreadLocal<ComplexObjectBuilder> builderThreadLocal;

    public void run() {
        // get the builder instance for this thread
        ComplexObjectBuilder builder = builderThreadLocal.get();
        // modify the builder state to create the object
        builder.setField1(1).setField2("value");
        // build the object
        ComplexObject obj = builder.build();
        // use the object
        // ...
    }
}
```

In this implementation, each client thread has its own instance of the ComplexObjectBuilder stored in a ThreadLocal variable called builderThreadLocal. The build() method of the builder is synchronized to ensure thread-safety when creating objects. Finally, the ComplexObject created by the builder is immutable, thus making it thread-safe for concurrent use without any additional synchronization.

5.11 Discuss the scalability and performance considerations when implementing the Facade pattern in a distributed or microservices architecture.

The Facade pattern is typically used to provide a simple and unified interface to a complex subsystem or set of functionality. In a distributed or microservices architecture, this can be particularly useful as it allows clients to interact with the system in a consistent and predictable manner, while shielding them from the complexity of the underlying components.

When implementing the Facade pattern in a distributed or microservices architecture, there are several key scalability and performance considerations that must be taken into account. These include:

1. Network Latency: When using the Facade pattern in a distributed architecture, each request must traverse the network between the client and the server, which can result in additional latency. This can be mitigated by minimizing the number of network round trips required, for example, by using caching or by batching requests.

2. Service Discovery: In a microservices architecture, service discovery is essential to enable components to locate and communicate with each other. This can be implemented using a variety of technologies, such as a service registry or a message broker. However, these technologies can introduce additional latency and complexity, so careful consideration must be given to their implementation.

3. Load Balancing: In a distributed architecture, multiple instances of a service may be running to handle incoming requests. To ensure that the load is balanced evenly between these instances, a load balancer can be used. However, this can introduce additional latency and may require more complex routing logic.

4. Scalability: As the number of clients and requests increases, the system must be able to scale to handle the additional load. This can be achieved through horizontal scaling, where additional instances of the service are added to handle the increased load, or through vertical scaling, where the resources allocated to each instance are increased.

5. Fault Tolerance: In a distributed architecture, components may fail, either due to hardware or software issues. To ensure that the system remains resilient to these failures, fault tolerance mechanisms must be implemented, such as redundancy, replication, or failover.

To illustrate these considerations, consider the following Java code example of a simple Facade pattern implementation in a distributed architecture. In this example, the Facade exposes a simple API for clients to retrieve weather data from a set of microservices that provide temperature, humidity, and wind speed information:

```java
public interface WeatherFacade {
    public WeatherData getWeatherData(String location);
}

public class WeatherFacadeImpl implements WeatherFacade {
    private TemperatureService temperatureService;
    private HumidityService humidityService;
    private WindService windService;

    public WeatherFacadeImpl(TemperatureService temperatureService,
        HumidityService humidityService, WindService windService) {
      this.temperatureService = temperatureService;
```

```
        this.humidityService = humidityService;
        this.windService = windService;
    }

    public WeatherData getWeatherData(String location) {
        float temperature = temperatureService.getTemperature(location)
            ;
        float humidity = humidityService.getHumidity(location);
        float windSpeed = windService.getWindSpeed(location);

        return new WeatherData(temperature, humidity, windSpeed);
    }
}

public interface TemperatureService {
    public float getTemperature(String location);
}

public class TemperatureServiceImpl implements TemperatureService {
    public float getTemperature(String location) {
        // Call to external temperature service
    }
}

public interface HumidityService {
    public float getHumidity(String location);
}

public class HumidityServiceImpl implements HumidityService {
    public float getHumidity(String location) {
        // Call to external humidity service
    }
}

public interface WindService {
    public float getWindSpeed(String location);
}

public class WindServiceImpl implements WindService {
    public float getWindSpeed(String location) {
        // Call to external wind speed service
    }
}
```

In this example, the WeatherFacadeImpl class serves as the
Facade to the underlying TemperatureService, HumidityService, and WindService microservices. When a client calls the
getWeatherData method on the Facade, it retrieves temperature, humidity, and wind speed data from each of the services

and returns a unified WeatherData object.

To ensure that this example is scalable and performant in a distributed architecture, several considerations must be taken into account. For example, the WeatherFacadeImpl class could use caching to minimize the number of network round trips required for each request, while the TemperatureService, HumidityService, and WindService classes could be deployed as separate microservices to enable horizontal scaling. Additionally, a load balancer could be used to evenly distribute incoming requests between multiple instances of each microservice, and fault tolerance mechanisms could be implemented to maintain system resilience in the face of component failures.

Overall, the Facade pattern can be a powerful tool when implemented in a distributed or microservices architecture, but it requires careful consideration of the scalability and performance implications in order to ensure that the system operates efficiently and reliably.

5.12   How can you apply the Chain of Responsibility pattern in a fault-tolerant system to ensure request processing even in case of partial system failures?

The Chain of Responsibility pattern is often used in software systems to handle requests in a flexible and extensible way. In a fault-tolerant system, we can apply this pattern to ensure request processing even in case of partial system failures.

The idea behind this pattern is to create a chain of handlers that receive a request and try to handle it. If a handler is unable to process the request, it passes the request to the next handler in the chain. This continues until either a handler successfully processes the request or the request reaches the end of the chain without being handled.

To apply this pattern in a fault-tolerant system, we can use a variation of the pattern called the CircuitBreaker pattern. The CircuitBreaker pattern is designed to handle faults and partial failures in distributed systems by opening a circuit when a service fails, and closing it when the service recovers.

In a fault-tolerant system, we can use the CircuitBreaker pattern to create a chain of handlers where each handler is responsible for handling a specific type of request. If a handler is unable to handle a request due to a partial system failure, it can open the circuit and pass the request to the next handler in the chain. The CircuitBreaker pattern is responsible for monitoring the health of the system and opening or closing circuits as needed.

Here's an example implementation of this pattern in Java:

```java
public abstract class RequestHandler {
    private RequestHandler nextHandler;
    private CircuitBreaker circuitBreaker;

    public void setNextHandler(RequestHandler handler) {
        this.nextHandler = handler;
    }

    public void setCircuitBreaker(CircuitBreaker circuitBreaker) {
        this.circuitBreaker = circuitBreaker;
    }

    public void handleRequest(Request request) {
        if (!circuitBreaker.isOpen()) {
            if (canHandle(request)) {
                handle(request);
            } else {
```

```
                if (nextHandler != null) {
                    nextHandler.handleRequest(request);
                } else {
                    circuitBreaker.open();
                }
            }
        }
    }

    protected abstract boolean canHandle(Request request);

    protected abstract void handle(Request request);
}

public class CircuitBreaker {
    private boolean open = false;

    public boolean isOpen() {
        return open;
    }

    public void open() {
        open = true;
    }

    public void close() {
        open = false;
    }
}

public class FaultTolerantSystem {
    private final RequestHandler firstHandler;

    public FaultTolerantSystem() {
        CircuitBreaker circuitBreaker = new CircuitBreaker();
        RequestHandler handler1 = new Handler1();
        RequestHandler handler2 = new Handler2();

        handler1.setCircuitBreaker(circuitBreaker);
        handler1.setNextHandler(handler2);
        handler2.setCircuitBreaker(circuitBreaker);

        firstHandler = handler1;
    }

    public void handleRequest(Request request) {
        firstHandler.handleRequest(request);
    }
}
```

In this example, we have an abstract 'RequestHandler' class
that defines the basic functionality for handling requests. Each

concrete handler subclass implements the 'canHandle' and 'handle' methods to determine if they can handle a request and to handle the request if they can.

The 'CircuitBreaker' class monitors the health of the system and opens or closes the circuit as needed. The 'FaultTolerantSystem' class initializes the handlers and sets up the chain of responsibility.

When a request is received by the 'FaultTolerantSystem', it is passed to the first handler in the chain. If the circuit is open due to a partial system failure, the request is not processed by any handler and the circuit remains open. If the request is successfully handled by a handler, the circuit remains closed. If the first handler cannot handle the request, it is passed to the next handler in the chain. This process continues until the request is successfully handled or the end of the chain is reached and the circuit is opened.

Overall, applying the Chain of Responsibility pattern with the CircuitBreaker pattern can help ensure request processing in a fault-tolerant system even in case of partial system failures.

5.13   Describe a scenario where the Composite pattern can be combined with the Iterator and Visitor patterns to traverse and manipulate complex object structures.

The Composite pattern can be used to create complex object structures where the objects can be composed of other objects of the same type. For example, consider a file system hierarchy where a directory can contain files and other sub-directories. The directory and file classes can be represented as composite objects, while the file system hierarchy can be represented as a tree structure.

To traverse and manipulate this tree structure, we can use the Iterator pattern to create an iterator that can visit each file and directory in the hierarchy. The Iterator pattern decouples the traversal logic from the underlying data structure, making it possible to iterate over different types of collections in a uniform way.

Furthermore, we can combine the Visitor pattern with the Iterator pattern to perform operations on the composite objects as they are being iterated over. For example, we may want to count the number of files or directories in the hierarchy, calculate the total size of all files, or perform some other operation that requires visiting every object in the hierarchy.

Here is an example Java code snippet that demonstrates this design:

```java
public interface FileSystemComponent {
  int getSize();
  void accept(FileSystemVisitor visitor);
  Iterator<FileSystemComponent> iterator();
}

public class File implements FileSystemComponent {
  private int size;

  public File(int size) {
    this.size = size;
  }

  public int getSize() {
    return size;
  }

  public void accept(FileSystemVisitor visitor) {
    visitor.visit(this);
```

```
    }
    public Iterator<FileSystemComponent> iterator() {
      return Collections.emptyIterator();
    }
  }

  public class Directory implements FileSystemComponent {
    private List<FileSystemComponent> components = new ArrayList<>();

    public void addComponent(FileSystemComponent component) {
      components.add(component);
    }

    public int getSize() {
      int size = 0;
      for (FileSystemComponent component : components) {
        size += component.getSize();
      }
      return size;
    }

    public void accept(FileSystemVisitor visitor) {
      visitor.visit(this);
      for (FileSystemComponent component : components) {
        component.accept(visitor);
      }
    }

    public Iterator<FileSystemComponent> iterator() {
      return components.iterator();
    }
  }

  public interface FileSystemVisitor {
    void visit(File file);
    void visit(Directory directory);
  }

  public class FileSystemCounter implements FileSystemVisitor {
    private int fileCount;
    private int directoryCount;

    public void visit(File file) {
      fileCount++;
    }

    public void visit(Directory directory) {
      directoryCount++;
    }

    public int getFileCount() {
      return fileCount;
    }
```

```
    public int getDirectoryCount() {
      return directoryCount;
    }
  }

  public class FileSystemSizeCalculator implements FileSystemVisitor {
    private int totalSize;

    public void visit(File file) {
      totalSize += file.getSize();
    }

    public void visit(Directory directory) {
      // Do nothing
    }

    public int getTotalSize() {
      return totalSize;
    }
  }
```

In this example, the 'FileSystemComponent' interface represents the composite objects in the file system hierarchy. The 'File' and 'Directory' classes are concrete implementations of this interface. The 'Directory' class contains a list of other 'FileSystemComponent' instances, which could be either files or directories.

The 'FileSystemVisitor' interface represents the operation that we want to perform on the composite objects. The 'FileSystem-Counter' and 'FileSystemSizeCalculator' classes are concrete implementations of this interface.

The 'accept' method on the 'FileSystemComponent' interface allows a 'FileSystemVisitor' to visit the composite object. The 'iterator' method returns an iterator that can traverse the object's children.

To count the number of files and directories, we can use the 'FileSystemCounter' class in the following way:

```
Directory root = new Directory();
```

```
root.addComponent(new File(10));
root.addComponent(new Directory());
root.addComponent(new File(20));

FileSystemCounter counter = new FileSystemCounter();
root.accept(counter);

System.out.println("Number␣of␣files:␣" + counter.getFileCount());
System.out.println("Number␣of␣directories:␣" + counter.
    getDirectoryCount());
```

To calculate the total size of all files, we can use the 'FileSystemSizeCalculator' class in the following way:

```
Directory root = new Directory();
Directory subdirectory = new Directory();
subdirectory.addComponent(new File(10));
subdirectory.addComponent(new File(20));
root.addComponent(subdirectory);
root.addComponent(new File(30));

FileSystemSizeCalculator sizeCalculator = new
    FileSystemSizeCalculator();
root.accept(sizeCalculator);

System.out.println("Total␣file␣size:␣" + sizeCalculator.getTotalSize
    ());
```

By using the Composite, Iterator, and Visitor patterns together, we can separate the traversal and operation logic, which makes it easier to manipulate complex object structures.

5.14 Discuss the implications of using the Flyweight pattern in a system with a large number of shared objects and high concurrency.

The Flyweight pattern is a structural design pattern that allows sharing of a large number of fine-grained objects efficiently. It is useful when there is a large number of instances and the cost of creating each instance is high. By sharing common attributes of those instances, the Flyweight pattern reduces the number of objects created and hence uses resources efficiently.

When it comes to a system with a large number of shared objects and high concurrency, there are several implications of using the Flyweight pattern.

Firstly, the Flyweight pattern can significantly reduce memory usage by sharing common attributes across multiple objects. In a high concurrency scenario, this can be especially important as it reduces the memory footprint of the system, and allows more objects to be loaded and updated in memory at the same time.

Secondly, using the Flyweight pattern can also improve performance by reducing the overhead of object creation. The creation and destruction of objects can be expensive, especially for complex objects. By allowing multiple objects to share common attributes, the Flyweight pattern can reduce the number of object creations and hence reduce the total overhead.

However, there are also some trade-offs to consider when using the Flyweight pattern in a highly concurrent system. The shared objects will have to be accessed in a thread-safe manner to avoid race conditions and other synchronization issues. This means that appropriate synchronization mechanisms, such as locks or atomic operations, will have to be put in place to ensure correct operation of the system.

Furthermore, if the shared objects are mutable, care must be taken to ensure that the state of an object is not modified by one thread while another thread is using it. This can be achieved

by either making the shared objects immutable or by ensuring
that all modifications are synchronized across all threads.

Java code example:

```java
public class FlyweightFactory {
    private Map<String, Flyweight> flyweights = new HashMap<>();

    public Flyweight getFlyweight(String key) {
        if (flyweights.containsKey(key)) {
            return flyweights.get(key);
        } else {
            Flyweight flyweight = new ConcreteFlyweight();
            flyweights.put(key, flyweight);
            return flyweight;
        }
    }
}

public interface Flyweight {
    void operation();
}

// ConcreteFlyweight that implements the Flyweight interface
public class ConcreteFlyweight implements Flyweight {
    @Override
    public void operation() {
        // Implement concrete operation
    }
}

// Client code that uses the FlyweightFactory to get shared Flyweight
//     objects
public class Client {
    private FlyweightFactory flyweightFactory = new FlyweightFactory
        ();

    public void doOperation(String key) {
        Flyweight flyweight = flyweightFactory.getFlyweight(key);
        flyweight.operation();
    }
}
```

In the above code example, the 'FlyweightFactory' maintains
a cache of shared 'Flyweight' objects that are retrieved by the
'Client' object. By sharing the 'Flyweight' objects, the system
can reduce its memory usage and reduce the overhead of object
creation. However, care must be taken to ensure that the ob-

jects are accessed and modified in a thread-safe manner in high concurrent systems.

5.15   Explain how the Mediator pattern can be implemented using event-driven architectures and message brokers like RabbitMQ or Apache Kafka.

The Mediator pattern is a behavioral design pattern that promotes loose coupling between objects by encapsulating their interactions within a mediator object. This reduces the dependencies between the objects, making the code more maintainable and scalable.

In an event-driven architecture, the Mediator pattern can be implemented using a message broker like RabbitMQ or Apache Kafka. When an event occurs, it is published to the broker, and the mediator subscribes to the relevant events. The mediator then processes the event, updating the relevant objects and publishing any changes back to the broker.

Here's an example of how the Mediator pattern can be implemented using RabbitMQ in Java:

1. Create a mediator object that subscribes to relevant events on the RabbitMQ broker:

```
public class Mediator {
    private final Channel channel;

    public Mediator(Channel channel) {
        this.channel = channel;
        try {
            channel.exchangeDeclare("events", BuiltinExchangeType.TOPIC)
```

```
      ;
    String queueName = channel.queueDeclare().getQueue();
    channel.queueBind(queueName, "events", "user.*");
    channel.basicConsume(queueName, true, this::processEvent,
        consumerTag -> {});
  } catch (IOException e) {
    throw new RuntimeException("Failed␣to␣create␣mediator", e);
  }
}

private void processEvent(Delivery delivery) throws IOException {
  String routingKey = delivery.getEnvelope().getRoutingKey();
  byte[] body = delivery.getBody();

  // Parse the event and update the relevant objects
  Event event = parseEvent(body);
  if (routingKey.startsWith("user.")) {
    int userId = Integer.parseInt(routingKey.substring(5));
    updateUser(userId, event);
  }
}

private void updateUser(int userId, Event event) {
  // Update the user object with the event data
  User user = getUser(userId);
  user.update(event);

  // Publish any changes back to the broker
  try {
    byte[] data = serializeUser(user);
    channel.basicPublish("users", "user." + userId, null, data);
  } catch (IOException e) {
    throw new RuntimeException("Failed␣to␣publish␣user", e);
  }
}
}
```

2. Create objects that subscribe to events on the mediator:

```
public class User {
  private final Mediator mediator;
  private final int id;
  // ...

  public User(Mediator mediator, int id) {
    this.mediator = mediator;
    this.id = id;
    mediator.subscribe("user." + id, this::onEvent);
  }

  private void onEvent(Event event) {
    // Handle the event
```

```
    }

    public void update(Event event) {
        // Update the user object with the event data
    }
}
```

3. Publish events to the RabbitMQ broker:

```
public class EventProducer {
    private final Channel channel;

    public EventProducer(Channel channel) {
        this.channel = channel;
        try {
            channel.exchangeDeclare("events", BuiltinExchangeType.TOPIC)
            ;
        } catch (IOException e) {
            throw new RuntimeException("Failed to create event producer"
                , e);
        }
    }

    public void publish(Event event, String routingKey) {
        try {
            byte[] data = serializeEvent(event);
            channel.basicPublish("events", routingKey, null, data);
        } catch (IOException e) {
            throw new RuntimeException("Failed to publish event", e);
        }
    }
}
```

With this implementation, objects can communicate with each
other indirectly through the mediator, reducing the coupling between them. Any changes to the objects are propagated through
the mediator and published back to the broker, ensuring consistency across the system.

5.16 Discuss the performance and security considerations when implementing the Proxy pattern for remote method invocation or virtual proxies.

The Proxy pattern is a structural design pattern that provides a surrogate, or placeholder, for another object to control access to it. In the case of remote method invocation, a proxy pattern is used to provide a local representation of a remote object to the client, which allows the client to interact with the remote object as if it were a local object. In the case of virtual proxies, a proxy pattern is used to delay the creation of an expensive object until it is actually needed.

When implementing a proxy pattern for remote method invocation or virtual proxies, there are several performance and security considerations to keep in mind.

Performance considerations:

- Network overhead: When using a proxy for remote method invocation, there is inevitably some network overhead involved in passing requests and responses to and from the remote object. This overhead can be minimized by using asynchronous messaging, caching frequently used data locally, and optimizing the network infrastructure.

- Latency: The use of a remote proxy can introduce latency into the system, particularly when the remote object is located far away from the client. This latency can be mitigated by reducing the amount of data that needs to be transmitted and optimizing the network infrastructure.

- Resource utilization: When using a virtual proxy, there is a risk that the actual object being represented will consume significant resources when it is finally instantiated. This risk can be mitigated by carefully monitoring resource utilization and ensuring that the object is only instantiated when it is absolutely necessary.

Security considerations:

- Authentication and authorization: When using a proxy for remote method invocation, it is important to ensure that the client is authenticated and authorized to make the request. This can be achieved by using secure authentication and authorization mechanisms, such as SSL/TLS, OAuth, or SAML.

- Encryption: To prevent sensitive data from being intercepted or compromised during transmission, it is critical to encrypt all traffic between the client and the remote object. This can be achieved by using secure encryption protocols, such as AES or RSA.

- Availability: A proxy can potentially become a single point of failure, particularly in a distributed system. To ensure availability, it is important to implement failover mechanisms, such as redundancy and load balancing, to ensure that clients can continue to access the remote object even in the event of a failure.

Here is an example of a Java code snippet that demonstrates the use of the Proxy pattern for remote method invocation:

```java
public interface RemoteService {
    public void doSomething();
}

public class RemoteServiceImpl implements RemoteService {
    public void doSomething() {
        // do something
    }
}

public class RemoteServiceProxy implements RemoteService {
    private String url;
    private RemoteService remoteService;

    public RemoteServiceProxy(String url) {
        this.url = url;
    }

    public void doSomething() {
```

```
        if (remoteService == null) {
            remoteService = (RemoteService) Naming.lookup(url);
        }
        remoteService.doSomething();
    }
}

public class Client {
    public static void main(String[] args) {
        RemoteService remoteService = new RemoteServiceProxy("rmi://
            localhost:1099/RemoteService");
        remoteService.doSomething();
    }
}
```

In this example, the 'RemoteService' interface defines the methods that can be invoked remotely, and the 'RemoteServiceImpl'
class implements those methods. The 'RemoteServiceProxy'
class acts as a surrogate for the 'RemoteServiceImpl' class and is
responsible for invoking the methods on the remote object. Finally, the 'Client' class uses the 'RemoteServiceProxy' to make
remote method invocations. By using this pattern, the client
can interact with the remote object as if it were a local object,
without having to worry about the underlying network infrastructure.

5.17 Describe a scenario where the Bridge pattern can be combined with the Prototype or Builder patterns to create highly configurable and extensible systems.

The Bridge pattern is used to separate the abstraction from its
implementation in order to allow them to vary independently.
This pattern is useful when you want to add new functionality

or change the implementation without changing the abstraction.

The Prototype pattern is used to create new objects based on a prototype copy, which is an efficient way to create multiple objects with the same attributes/properties. The Builder pattern is used to create complex objects using a step-by-step approach.

One scenario where the Bridge pattern can be combined with the Prototype or Builder patterns is creating a highly configurable and extensible system that involves different messaging protocols such as TCP, HTTP or FTP. In this scenario, we can apply the Bridge pattern to separate the Message abstraction from its implementation, so we could easily switch between different messaging protocols without affecting the Message abstraction.

To create highly configurable and extensible systems, we can use the Prototype or Builder pattern to create different types of messages based on some configurations. For example, we could have a configuration file that specifies the message type, the protocol, and other options. Then, we can use the Prototype pattern to create a prototype message based on the configuration, which can be used to create multiple objects with the same configuration.

Here's how we can implement this scenario in Java, using the Bridge, Prototype, and Builder patterns:

First, we define the Message interface and its implementation using the Bridge pattern:

```
public interface Message {
    void send();
}
```

```
public abstract class AbstractMessage implements Message {
    protected MessageSender sender;
    protected String message;

    public AbstractMessage(String message, MessageSender sender) {
        this.message = message;
        this.sender = sender;
    }
}
```

Next, we implement different message senders:

```
public interface MessageSender {
    void sendMessage(String message);
}

public class TcpMessageSender implements MessageSender {
    public void sendMessage(String message) {
        // Implementation
    }
}

public class HttpMessageSender implements MessageSender {
    public void sendMessage(String message) {
        // Implementation
    }
}

public class FtpMessageSender implements MessageSender {
    public void sendMessage(String message) {
        // Implementation
    }
}
```

Now, we can use the Builder pattern to create different types
of messages based on some configurations:

```
public interface MessageBuilder {
    MessageBuilder setProtocol(String protocol);
    MessageBuilder setFrom(String from);
    MessageBuilder setTo(String to);
    MessageBuilder setSubject(String subject);
    MessageBuilder setText(String text);

    Message build();
}

public class EmailMessageBuilder implements MessageBuilder {
    private EmailMessage message;
```

```java
    public EmailMessageBuilder() {
        this.message = new EmailMessage();
    }

    public MessageBuilder setProtocol(String protocol) {
        // Implementation for email protocol
        return this;
    }

    public MessageBuilder setFrom(String from) {
        this.message.setFrom(from);
        return this;
    }

    public MessageBuilder setTo(String to) {
        this.message.setTo(to);
        return this;
    }

    public MessageBuilder setSubject(String subject) {
        this.message.setSubject(subject);
        return this;
    }

    public MessageBuilder setText(String text) {
        this.message.setText(text);
        return this;
    }

    public Message build() {
        return this.message.clone();
    }
}

public class EmailMessage extends AbstractMessage implements
    Cloneable {
    private String from;
    private String to;
    private String subject;
    private String text;

    public EmailMessage() {
        super("", null);
    }

    public void send() {
        this.sender.sendMessage(message);
    }

    public void setFrom(String from) {
        this.from = from;
    }

    public void setTo(String to) {
        this.to = to;
    }
```

```
public void setSubject(String subject) {
    this.subject = subject;
}

public void setText(String text) {
    this.text = text;
}

@Override
public EmailMessage clone() {
    return new EmailMessage(this.from, this.to, this.subject,
        this.text, this.sender);
}

public EmailMessage(String from, String to, String subject,
    String text, MessageSender sender) {
    super("", sender);
    this.from = from;
    this.to = to;
    this.subject = subject;
    this.text = text;
    this.message = "From:␣" + from + "n"
            + "To:␣" + to + "n"
            + "Subject:␣" + subject + "n"
            + text;
    }
}
```

We can define other builders for different types of messages and protocols, and also use the Prototype pattern to clone existing messages with different configurations rather than creating a new one from scratch.

This approach creates a highly configurable and extensible system that can support different messaging protocols and configurations without affecting the Message abstraction. It also provides a flexible way to create multiple messages with the same configuration using the Prototype pattern, or create complex messages step-by-step using the Builder pattern.

5.18   Explain how the Template Method pattern can be adapted to support the parallel execution of sub-tasks within an algorithm.

The Template Method pattern is a behavioral design pattern that defines the skeleton of an algorithm in a superclass, but lets subclasses override specific steps of the algorithm without changing its structure. The idea behind the Template Method is to let subclasses implement individual steps of an algorithm without letting them change the algorithm's structure.

Parallelization is a method of improving the performance of an algorithm by breaking down a large task into smaller subtasks that can be executed simultaneously. In order to support parallel execution of sub-tasks within an algorithm, the Template Method pattern can be adapted in the following way:

1. Identify the steps in the algorithm that can be executed in parallel. These steps should be independent of each other and not rely on the output of other steps.

2. Modify the Template Method to use parallel streams for executing the parallelizable steps. Parallel streams are a feature in Java that allows for parallel execution of collections.

3. Create a new abstract method in the superclass that returns the collection of sub-tasks that can be executed in parallel.

4. Implement the new abstract method in the subclass to return a collection of sub-tasks that can be executed in parallel.

5. Override the parallelizable steps in the subclass to execute

them in parallel using the parallel streams.

Here is an example of how the Template Method pattern can be adapted to support parallel execution of sub-tasks within an algorithm:

```java
// Abstract superclass with the Template Method
public abstract class Algorithm {
    // ...
    public void execute() {
        // Step 1
        step1();

        // Step 2: parallelizable steps
        Collection<SubTask> subTasks = getParallelizableSubTasks();
        subTasks.parallelStream().forEach(SubTask::execute);

        // Step 3
        step3();
    }

    protected abstract Collection<SubTask> getParallelizableSubTasks
        ();

    protected void step1() {
        // Default implementation
    }

    protected void step3() {
        // Default implementation
    }
}

// Subclass that implements the parallelizable sub-tasks
public class ParallelAlgorithm extends Algorithm {
    // ...
    @Override
    protected Collection<SubTask> getParallelizableSubTasks() {
        Collection<SubTask> subTasks = new ArrayList<>();
        subTasks.add(new SubTask());
        subTasks.add(new SubTask());
        return subTasks;
    }

    // Override the parallelizable steps to execute them in parallel
    @Override
    protected void step2() {
        Collection<SubTask> subTasks = getParallelizableSubTasks();
        subTasks.parallelStream().forEach(SubTask::execute);
    }
}
```

In this example, the 'Algorithm' class defines the Template Method with steps 1, 2, and 3. Step 2 is the parallelizable step, which is modified to use a collection of sub-tasks that can be executed in parallel. The 'getParallelizableSubTasks()' method is defined as abstract in the superclass, and its implementation is provided in the subclass. The 'step2()' method is overridden in the subclass to execute the sub-tasks in parallel using the 'parallelStream()' method.

By adapting the Template Method pattern in this way, we can support parallel execution of sub-tasks within an algorithm and improve its performance.

5.19 Discuss the impact of using the Abstract Factory pattern on a system's complexity and how it can be mitigated using other structural patterns like the Module or Facade patterns.

The 'Abstract Factory' pattern is a creational pattern used to provide a way to create families of related objects without specifying their concrete classes. The pattern defines an abstract class that declares factory methods, which return instances of the abstract product classes. The concrete classes for these product classes are implemented by the different factories.

One of the benefits of using the 'Abstract Factory' pattern is that it helps to decouple the client code from the concrete classes of the objects it uses. By using an abstract class to define the interface that the client code interacts with, the client code is not dependent on the concrete classes of the objects. This makes it possible to easily switch to a different implementation of the objects without having to change the client code.

However, using the 'Abstract Factory' pattern can also increase the complexity of the system. The creation of objects is delegated to a set of factories, which can result in a large number of classes being used to construct the objects. This can make the system more difficult to understand and maintain.

To mitigate the complexity introduced by the 'Abstract Factory' pattern, other structural patterns can be used. Two such patterns are the 'Module' and 'Facade' patterns:

- 'Module Pattern': This pattern helps to organize the code by grouping related components together into loosely coupled modules. Each module has an interface that defines the operations it supports and hides the implementation details from other modules. By using the 'Module' pattern, it becomes possible to organize the factories into separate modules based on their functionality, which helps to reduce the complexity of the system.

- 'Facade Pattern': This pattern provides a simplified interface to a complex system. It defines a higher-level interface that makes it easier for the client code to interact with the system by hiding the implementation details. By using the 'Facade' pattern, it is possible to hide the details of the 'Abstract Factory' pattern and provide a simpler interface to the client code.

Here is an example of using the 'Abstract Factory' pattern with the 'Module' and 'Facade' patterns to help mitigate complexity:

```
// Abstract factory class
interface WidgetFactory {
```

```
    Button createButton();
    TextField createTextField();
}

// Concrete factory implementing WidgetFactory
class MacWidgetFactory implements WidgetFactory {
    Button createButton() {
        return new MacButton();
    }
    TextField createTextField() {
        return new MacTextField();
    }
}

// Concrete factory implementing WidgetFactory
class WindowsWidgetFactory implements WidgetFactory {
    Button createButton() {
        return new WindowsButton();
    }
    TextField createTextField() {
        return new WindowsTextField();
    }
}

// Abstract product class
interface Button {
    void render();
}

// Concrete product class implementing Button
class MacButton implements Button {
    void render() {
        System.out.println("Rendering Mac button");
    }
}

// Concrete product class implementing Button
class WindowsButton implements Button {
    void render() {
        System.out.println("Rendering Windows button");
    }
}

// Abstract product class
interface TextField {
    void render();
}

// Concrete product class implementing TextField
class MacTextField implements TextField {
    void render() {
        System.out.println("Rendering Mac text field");
    }
```

```
}

// Concrete product class implementing TextField
class WindowsTextField implements TextField {
    void render() {
        System.out.println("Rendering Windows text field");
    }
}

// Module that groups related factories together
class WidgetModule {
    static WidgetFactory createWidgetFactory(String type) {
        if (type.equals("mac")) {
            return new MacWidgetFactory();
        } else if (type.equals("windows")) {
            return new WindowsWidgetFactory();
        } else {
            throw new IllegalArgumentException("Invalid widget type");
        }
    }
}

// Facade that provides a simplified interface to the system
class WidgetFacade {
    static void renderButton(String type) {
        WidgetFactory factory = WidgetModule.createWidgetFactory(type
            );
        Button button = factory.createButton();
        button.render();
    }

    static void renderTextField(String type) {
        WidgetFactory factory = WidgetModule.createWidgetFactory(type
            );
        TextField textField = factory.createTextField();
        textField.render();
    }
}
```

In this example, the 'Abstract Factory' pattern is used to create families of related objects ('Button' and 'TextField') without specifying their concrete classes. Two factories are provided ('WindowsWidgetFactory' and 'MacWidgetFactory') to create the objects. The 'Module' pattern is used to group the factories together based on their functionality. The 'WidgetFacade' serves as a simplified interface to the system, hiding the details of the factories and making it simple for the client code to ren-

der the widgets ('Button' and 'TextField') without interacting
with the factories directly.

5.20   Explain how the Visitor pattern can be adapted to support asynchronous operations, and discuss the implications on the overall performance and responsiveness of the system.

The Visitor pattern, at its core, allows for operations to be
performed on a complex hierarchical structure of objects without having to clutter the objects with additional functionality.
However, in the classic implementation of the Visitor pattern,
the operations are performed synchronously, meaning that the
program waits for the completion of the operation before con-
tinuing execution.

In many scenarios, especially those involving large datasets
or input/output operations, synchronous execution can cause
unacceptable delays in system responsiveness. To avoid such
delays, the Visitor pattern can be adapted to allow for asynchronous execution, in which the program can continue to execute while the operation is being performed in the background.

The adapted version of the Visitor pattern would use asynchronous callback functions to signal the completion of the
operation. In particular, each visit operation in the Visitor
class would take an additional callback function as an argument, which would be invoked when the operation is complete.
This way, the Visitor can return immediately after starting the

operation, allowing other parts of the program to run in the meantime.

Here is an example implementation of a simple asynchronous Visitor pattern in Java:

```
public interface AsyncVisitor<T> {
    void visit(T obj, AsyncCallback callback);
}

public interface AsyncCallback {
    void onComplete();
}

public class AsyncPrinter<T> implements AsyncVisitor<T> {
    public void visit(T obj, AsyncCallback callback) {
        // Perform the printing in a separate thread
        new Thread(() -> {
            System.out.println(obj);
            // Signal the completion of the operation
            callback.onComplete();
        }).start();
    }
}
```

In this example, the 'AsyncVisitor' interface defines the visit operation with an additional callback argument, and the 'AsyncPrinter' class is an implementation of this interface that performs printing asynchronously in a separate thread.

The use of asynchronous Visitor pattern can significantly improve the performance and responsiveness of the system by allowing the program to continue execution while the long-running operations are being performed in the background. However, care must be taken to avoid performance issues caused by too many concurrent operations, as well as potential synchronization issues when accessing shared resources. Therefore, proper design and testing are required to ensure the reliability and efficiency of the system.

Chapter 6

Guru

6.1 Discuss the impact of design patterns on the overall architecture of a system, including how patterns can influence modularity, maintainability, and scalability.

Design patterns are reusable solutions to commonly occurring software problems. They provide a general framework and templates for solving a specific set of problems. Design patterns influence the overall architecture of a system in several ways. First, they provide a set of guidelines for organizing the system's components, promoting modularity and enhancing the code reusability. Second, patterns promote maintainability by isolating changes to a specific component, thus avoiding ripple effects throughout the system. Finally, they facilitate the scalability of the system by enabling the dynamic allocation of resources.

One of the primary ways that design patterns impact the overall architecture of a system is by promoting modularity. A modular system is one that is divided into independent parts that can interact with each other through well-defined interfaces. Design patterns provide templates for building such modules, based on a set of principles and practices that have been tried and tested in large-scale systems.

For example, the Factory Method design pattern promotes modularity by defining a single interface for creating objects. This interface provides a standard way of creating objects regardless of their implementation, enabling the system to remain modular even when the implementation changes. Similarly, the Observer design pattern promotes modularity by defining a set of events that can be observed by an arbitrary number of observers, without any knowledge or coupling between them.

Design patterns also promote maintainability by isolating changes to a specific component, avoiding ripple effects throughout the system. Because design patterns are well-defined and their implementation is encapsulated, updates and modifications to a specific pattern do not affect the functionality of other patterns. This ability to isolate changes facilitates maintenance, reduces costs, and allows for greater flexibility in changing the system.

For instance, if a specific business rule changes in a system that uses the Template Method design pattern, the changes can be made in one subclass without affecting the behavior of other subclasses. Similarly, if a system that uses the Adapter pattern needs to interface with a new external system, a new adapter can be created without having to modify existing code.

Finally, design patterns facilitate the scalability of the system by enabling the dynamic allocation of resources. Scalability refers to the ability of a system to grow in size and complexity over time, and design patterns offer a set of solutions for dealing with this challenge. For example, the Singleton design pattern ensures that there is only one instance of a class, promoting efficient use of resources. Similarly, the Iterator design pattern enables efficient traversal through large collections of data, maximizing performance and scalability.

In conclusion, design patterns play a crucial role in determining the architecture of a system. They promote modularity, maintainability, and scalability, helping developers create more flexible, efficient, and robust systems. By providing reusable templates for solving common software problems, design patterns enable developers to focus on high-level design instead of low-level implementation, saving time and effort while improving the overall quality of the code.

6.2 Explain how the Factory Method pattern and the Abstract Factory pattern can be combined with other creational patterns like Singleton, Prototype, or Builder to address specific architectural challenges.

The Factory Method pattern and the Abstract Factory pattern are creational design patterns that enable the creation of objects in different ways. These patterns provide a way to encapsulate the object creation process and make it easier to exchange implementations without affecting client code. These patterns can be combined with other creational patterns like Singleton, Prototype, or Builder to address specific architectural challenges.

Factory Method pattern with Singleton pattern

The Factory Method pattern can be combined with the Singleton pattern to ensure that only one instance of a factory object is created in the entire application. This can be useful in situations where multiple objects of a certain type need to be created but only one factory object is needed. In this pattern combination, the Singleton pattern is used to ensure that only one instance of the factory is created and the Factory Method pattern is used to create the objects. The following Java code example shows how this pattern combination can be implemented:

```java
public class MySingletonFactory {
    private static MySingletonFactory instance = null;

    private MySingletonFactory() {}

    public static MySingletonFactory getInstance() {
        if (instance == null) {
            instance = new MySingletonFactory();
        }
        return instance;
    }

    public MyObject createMyObject() {
        return new MyObject();
    }
}
```

Abstract Factory pattern with Singleton pattern

The Abstract Factory pattern can also be combined with the Singleton pattern to ensure that only one instance of an abstract factory object is created in the entire application. This can be useful in situations where multiple families of related objects

need to be created but only one instance of each factory is
needed. In this pattern combination, the Singleton pattern is
used to ensure that only one instance of the abstract factory
is created and the Abstract Factory pattern is used to create
the families of objects. The following Java code example shows
how this pattern combination can be implemented:

```java
public abstract class AbstractMyFactory {
    public abstract MyObject createMyObject();
}

public class MyFactory extends AbstractMyFactory {
    private static MyFactory instance = null;

    private MyFactory() {}

    public static MyFactory getInstance() {
        if (instance == null) {
            instance = new MyFactory();
        }
        return instance;
    }

    public MyObject createMyObject() {
        return new MyObject();
    }
}
```

Abstract Factory pattern with Prototype pattern

The Abstract Factory pattern can be combined with the Prototype pattern to enable the creation of new objects by copying
existing objects. This can be useful in situations where multiple
families of related objects need to be created and each family
has slightly different configurations. In this pattern combination, the Prototype pattern is used to create a prototype object
and the Abstract Factory pattern is used to create the families
of objects by copying the prototype object and making slight
modifications. The following Java code example shows how this
pattern combination can be implemented:

```java
public abstract class AbstractMyFactory {
```

```
    public abstract MyObject createMyObject();
}

public class MyObject implements Cloneable {
    // implementation of MyObject
    public MyObject clone() {
        return super.clone();
    }
}

public class MyFactory extends AbstractMyFactory {
    private MyObject prototype = new MyObject();

    public MyObject createMyObject() {
        MyObject newObject = prototype.clone();
        // make modifications to newObject if necessary
        return newObject;
    }
}
```

Builder pattern with Abstract Factory pattern and Prototype pattern

The Builder pattern can be combined with the Abstract Factory pattern and the Prototype pattern to enable the creation of complex objects with different configurations. This can be useful in situations where multiple families of related objects need to be created and each family has complex configurations. In this pattern combination, the Abstract Factory pattern is used to create the families of prototype objects, the Prototype pattern is used to create a prototype of each complex object, and the Builder pattern is used to build the final objects by copying the prototype and using the builder to modify the object's configuration. The following Java code example shows how this pattern combination can be implemented:

```
public abstract class AbstractMyFactory {
    public abstract MyObjectPrototype createMyObjectPrototype();
}

public interface MyObjectPrototype extends Cloneable {
    MyObjectPrototype clone();
    void setProperty1(Property1 property1);
```

```
    void setProperty2(Property2 property2);
    // other setter methods for properties
    MyObject build();
}

public class MyObject implements Serializable {
    // implementation of MyObject
}

public class MyObjectPrototypeImpl implements MyObjectPrototype {
    private MyObject object = new MyObject();
    private Property1 property1 = null;
    private Property2 property2 = null;
    // other properties

    public void setProperty1(Property1 property1) {
        this.property1 = property1;
    }

    public void setProperty2(Property2 property2) {
        this.property2 = property2;
    }

    public MyObjectPrototype clone() {
        MyObjectPrototypeImpl newPrototype = new
            MyObjectPrototypeImpl();
        newPrototype.object = this.object.clone();
        newPrototype.property1 = this.property1.clone();
        newPrototype.property2 = this.property2.clone();
        // other properties
        return newPrototype;
    }

    public MyObject build() {
        // set properties on object
        object.setProperty1(property1);
        object.setProperty2(property2);
        // other properties
        return object;
    }
}

public class MyObjectBuilder {
    private MyObjectPrototype prototype;

    public MyObjectBuilder(AbstractMyFactory factory) {
        prototype = factory.createMyObjectPrototype();
    }

    public void setProperty1(Property1 property1) {
        prototype.setProperty1(property1);
    }

    public void setProperty2(Property2 property2) {
        prototype.setProperty2(property2);
```

```
    }
    // other setter methods
    public MyObject build() {
        return prototype.build();
    }
}
```

In conclusion, there are many ways to combine creational design patterns to address specific architectural challenges. The combination of patterns will depend on the requirements of the application and the design goals of the architecture.

6.3   Describe how the Observer pattern can be implemented with distributed event streaming platforms, such as Apache Kafka or Amazon Kinesis, to support event-driven architectures at scale.

The Observer pattern is a design pattern where an object, called the subject, maintains a list of its dependents, called observers, and notifies them automatically of any state changes. Distributed event streaming platforms, such as Apache Kafka or Amazon Kinesis, are commonly used to implement event-driven architectures, where applications communicate with each other through events. In this architecture, the Observer pattern can be implemented with these platforms to support event-driven systems at scale.

To implement the Observer pattern with a distributed event streaming platform, the following steps can be taken:

1. A subject application should be configured to publish events to a topic on the event streaming platform.

2. Multiple observer applications should be configured to subscribe to the topic on the event streaming platform to receive events.

3. Each observer application should maintain its own state, based on the events it receives.

4. When the subject application publishes an event to the topic, all observer applications subscribed to the topic should receive the event.

5. Each observer application should update its own state based on the event it received.

By implementing the Observer pattern with a distributed event streaming platform, applications can be designed to be highly scalable and resilient. For example, multiple instances of the subject and observer applications can be deployed to handle high volumes of events and provide fault tolerance. Additionally, the event streaming platform can enable applications to process events in real-time, improving the overall system's agility and responsiveness.

Here is an example implementation of the Observer pattern using Apache Kafka in Java:

```java
// Subject class
public class KafkaEventSubject {

    private Producer<String, String> producer;
    private String topicName;

    public KafkaEventSubject(String topicName) {
        Properties configProperties = new Properties();
        configProperties.put(ProducerConfig.BOOTSTRAP_SERVERS_CONFIG,
            "localhost:9092");
```

```java
            configProperties.put(ProducerConfig.
                KEY_SERIALIZER_CLASS_CONFIG, StringSerializer.class.
                getName());
            configProperties.put(ProducerConfig.
                VALUE_SERIALIZER_CLASS_CONFIG, StringSerializer.class.
                getName());
            this.topicName = topicName;
            this.producer = new KafkaProducer<>(configProperties);
        }

    public void publishEvent(String event) {
        ProducerRecord<String, String> record = new ProducerRecord<>(
            this.topicName, event);
        producer.send(record, new Callback() {
            @Override
            public void onCompletion(RecordMetadata metadata,
                Exception e) {
                if (e != null) {
                    e.printStackTrace();
                }
                System.out.println("Event produced: " + event);
            }
        });
    }
}

// Observer class
public class KafkaEventListener {

    private KafkaConsumer<String, String> consumer;
    private String topicName;

    public KafkaEventListener(String topicName) {
        Properties properties = new Properties();
        properties.put(ConsumerConfig.BOOTSTRAP_SERVERS_CONFIG, "
            localhost:9092");
        properties.put(ConsumerConfig.KEY_DESERIALIZER_CLASS_CONFIG,
            StringDeserializer.class.getName());
        properties.put(ConsumerConfig.VALUE_DESERIALIZER_CLASS_CONFIG
            , StringDeserializer.class.getName());
        properties.put(ConsumerConfig.GROUP_ID_CONFIG, "group1");
        properties.put(ConsumerConfig.AUTO_OFFSET_RESET_CONFIG, "
            earliest");
        this.topicName = topicName;
        this.consumer = new KafkaConsumer<>(properties);
    }

    public void startListening() {
        consumer.subscribe(Collections.singletonList(topicName));
        while (true) {
            ConsumerRecords<String, String> records = consumer.poll(
                Duration.ofSeconds(1));
            for (ConsumerRecord<String, String> record : records) {
                System.out.println("Event consumed: " + record.value()
```

```
            );
        // update state based on the event
        }
      }
    }
}

// Example usage
public static void main(String[] args) {
    KafkaEventSubject subject = new KafkaEventSubject("eventsTopic")
        ;
    KafkaEventListener observer1 = new KafkaEventListener("
        eventsTopic");
    KafkaEventListener observer2 = new KafkaEventListener("
        eventsTopic");

    observer1.startListening();
    observer2.startListening();

    subject.publishEvent("Event␣1");
    subject.publishEvent("Event␣2");
}
```

In this example, the 'KafkaEventSubject' class publishes events
to the 'eventsTopic' topic, and the 'KafkaEventListener' class
listens for events on the same topic. Multiple instances of
'KafkaEventListener' can be created to behave as observers.
When an event is published, all observers subscribed to the
topic will receive the event and update their state accordingly.

6.4 Analyze the trade-offs between the Decorator pattern and Aspect-Oriented Programming (AOP) when it comes to handling cross-cutting concerns in a large-scale application.

Cross-cutting concerns are aspects of a software system that affect multiple modules and functions, and they are generally dif-

ficult to modularize and isolate. Examples of cross-cutting concerns include logging, caching, security, and transaction management. Two common techniques for handling cross-cutting concerns in a large-scale application are the Decorator pattern and Aspect-Oriented Programming (AOP). In this answer, we will analyze the trade-offs between these two techniques.

Decorator Pattern

The Decorator pattern is a structural pattern that allows behavior to be added to an individual object, either statically or dynamically, without affecting the behavior of other objects of the same class. The Decorator pattern involves creating multiple concrete classes that implement a common interface, and each of these concrete classes adds extra functionality to the wrapped object.

The Decorator pattern is good for handling cross-cutting concerns because it allows new behavior to be added to an object without modifying its existing behavior. Thus, the existing code base is less likely to be affected, and the additional behavior can be selectively and incrementally added to particular objects or object hierarchies. This can make debugging and maintenance easier, as changes to one object will not affect others.

Here is an example of how the Decorator pattern can be used to handle logging:

```java
public interface Service {
  void doSomething();
}

public class BasicService implements Service {
  public void doSomething() {
    System.out.println("BasicService.doSomething()");
  }
```

```
}

public class LoggingDecorator implements Service {
  private Service decoratedService;

  public LoggingDecorator(Service decoratedService) {
    this.decoratedService = decoratedService;
  }

  public void doSomething() {
    System.out.println("LoggingDecorator:␣entering␣doSomething()");
    decoratedService.doSomething();
    System.out.println("LoggingDecorator:␣exiting␣doSomething()");
  }
}
```

In this example, the 'BasicService' class is the base class that implements the 'Service' interface, and the 'LoggingDecorator' class is a concrete class that also implements the 'Service' interface, but delegates the actual implementation to another 'Service' object, which it takes in its constructor. The 'LoggingDecorator' adds logging behavior before and after calling the 'doSomething()' method of the decorated service.

Aspect-Oriented Programming (AOP)

AOP is a programming paradigm that allows cross-cutting concerns to be modularized and decoupled from the core logic of an application. In AOP, cross-cutting concerns are represented as "aspects", which are modular units of behavior that can be applied to other parts of the application without modifying their code directly. AOP involves two main concepts: "join points", which are points in the application where an aspect can be applied, and "advice", which is the behavior that is executed when an aspect is applied to a join point.

AOP frameworks like Spring AOP provide a way to declaratively specify join points and advice using annotations or XML configuration files. AOP also supports "pointcut expressions",

which allow developers to specify a set of join points based on
method signatures, classes, annotations, and other criteria.

AOP has several advantages over the Decorator pattern for handling cross-cutting concerns. First, AOP allows cross-cutting
concerns to be modularized and reused across multiple modules and functions, reducing code duplication and promoting
code organization. Second, AOP allows cross-cutting concerns
to be selectively applied to join points, making it more flexible than the Decorator pattern, which requires a new concrete
class for each combination of base behavior and added behavior. Third, AOP allows cross-cutting concerns to be applied to
multiple objects, making it more scalable than the Decorator
pattern, which requires a new object for each instance of added
behavior.

Here is an example of how AOP can be used to handle logging
using Spring AOP:

```
@Aspect
public class LoggingAspect {
  @Before("execution(* com.example.service.*.*(..))")
  public void logMethodEntry(JoinPoint joinPoint) {
    String methodName = joinPoint.getSignature().getName();
    String className = joinPoint.getTarget().getClass().
        getSimpleName();
    System.out.println("Entering " + className + "." + methodName);
  }

  @AfterReturning(pointcut = "execution(* com.example.service
      .*.*(..))",
            returning = "result")
  public void logMethodExit(JoinPoint joinPoint, Object result) {
    String methodName = joinPoint.getSignature().getName();
    String className = joinPoint.getTarget().getClass().
        getSimpleName();
    System.out.println("Exiting " + className + "." + methodName +
            ", returning " + result);
  }
}
```

In this example, we use the '@Aspect' annotation to mark the 'LoggingAspect' class as an aspect, and we define two advice methods, 'logMethodEntry()' and 'logMethodExit()', using the '@Before' and '@AfterReturning' annotations, respectively. We use a "pointcut expression" to specify that these advice methods should be applied to all methods in the 'com.example.service' package. When one of these methods is executed, the 'Join-Point' parameter contains information about the method that was called, which we can use to generate logging output.

Trade-offs

The Decorator pattern and AOP have different trade-offs depending on the requirements of the application.

- **Modularity**: AOP promotes modularity by allowing cross-cutting concerns to be modularized and decoupled from the core logic of an application. The Decorator pattern promotes modularity by allowing behavior to be selectively added to an object, without modifying its existing behavior. Both techniques can reduce code duplication and improve code organization.

- **Flexibility**: AOP is more flexible than the Decorator pattern, because it allows cross-cutting concerns to be selectively applied to join points using pointcut expressions. The Decorator pattern requires a new concrete class for each combination of base behavior and added behavior. AOP allows cross-cutting concerns to be applied to any join point, regardless of the base behavior.

- **Scalability**: AOP is more scalable than the Decorator pattern, because it allows cross-cutting concerns to be applied to multiple objects, without requiring a new object for each instance of added behavior. The Decorator pattern requires a new object for each instance of added behavior.

- **Performance**: The Decorator pattern can have a performance overhead, because each object is wrapped by multiple layers of decorators, which can introduce additional function calls and memory allocations. AOP can also have a performance overhead, because it involves intercepting method calls and executing advice methods, which can introduce additional method calls and object allocations. Both techniques can be optimized to minimize the performance overhead, but the performance requirements of the application should be considered.

In summary, the Decorator pattern and AOP are both useful techniques for handling cross-cutting concerns in a large-scale application. The Decorator pattern is good for selective and incremental addition of behavior, while AOP is good for modularization and reuse of behavior. The selection between the two should be done according to the specific requirements of the application.

6.5 Discuss the implications of using the Strategy pattern in a microservices architecture, considering factors such as deployment, versioning, and service discovery.

The Strategy pattern is a behavioral design pattern that allows an object to alter its behavior at runtime by selecting a different algorithm. In a microservices architecture, the Strategy pattern can be used to decouple the algorithmic logic of a service from its implementation, providing greater flexibility and extensibility for the service.

However, the adoption of the Strategy pattern in a microservices architecture brings about additional challenges, especially in the areas of deployment, versioning, and service discovery.

Deployment: As each microservice is developed independently, the adoption of the Strategy pattern may result in multiple versions of the same algorithm being deployed across different services. This can increase the complexity of deployment and potentially lead to version incompatibilities between services.

Versioning: Versioning of the microservices becomes more complicated when the Strategy pattern is used. If changes are made to the algorithmic logic, it may be necessary to modify the API and version the service to avoid compatibility issues with the client applications.

Service discovery: Since the algorithmic logic in the form of a Strategy can be used by multiple services, it becomes more difficult to discover which services are using which Strategy. Additional metadata or documentation may be necessary to enable service discovery in this scenario.

To address these challenges, a few best practices can be followed:

1. Standardize the use of algorithms across services to minimize versioning conflicts.

2. Use a centralized repository for the Strategies to ensure consistency and avoid duplication.

3. Implement a clear and consistent versioning strategy that is communicated to all stakeholders.

4. Utilize service discovery tools that provide metadata and documentation to enable automated discovery and integration of the services.

Here is an example of how the Strategy pattern can be imple-

mented in Java using an interface and concrete classes for the
Strategies:

```java
public interface PaymentStrategy {
  void pay(double amount);
}

public class CreditCardStrategy implements PaymentStrategy {

  private String cardNumber;
  private String cvv;
  private String expiryDate;

  public CreditCardStrategy(String cardNumber, String cvv, String
      expiryDate) {
    this.cardNumber = cardNumber;
    this.cvv = cvv;
    this.expiryDate = expiryDate;
  }

  @Override
  public void pay(double amount) {
    // conduct payment using credit card details
  }
}

public class PayPalStrategy implements PaymentStrategy {

  private String email;
  private String password;

  public PayPalStrategy(String email, String password) {
    this.email = email;
    this.password = password;
  }

  @Override
  public void pay(double amount) {
    // conduct payment using PayPal account
  }
}
```

In this example, the 'PaymentStrategy' interface defines the behavior for the payment strategy. The 'CreditCardStrategy' and
'PayPalStrategy' classes implement the 'PaymentStrategy' interface with their own algorithm for conducting payments. The
choice of which strategy to use can be determined at runtime,
providing flexibility for the system.

6.6 Explain how the State pattern can be used to model and manage complex workflows, such as business process management (BPM) or stateful microservices.

The State design pattern allows objects to change their behavior depending on their internal state. This pattern is useful in modeling and managing complex workflows, such as business process management (BPM) or stateful microservices.

When applied to BPM, the State pattern allows for the modeling of complex workflows with multiple states and transitions between them. Each state represents a specific stage in the workflow, and each transition represents a change from one state to another. By using this pattern, we can decouple the state management from the business logic, allowing for easier maintenance and extension.

Similarly, in stateful microservices, the State pattern can be used to manage the internal state of the microservice. As the service interacts with external systems, its internal state will change, and its behavior will need to be adapted accordingly. The State pattern can be used to model this behavior, allowing for easier maintenance and extension of the service.

Let's look at an example of how the State pattern can be used in BPM:

Suppose we have a workflow for processing a loan application. The workflow starts with the state "Received", then moves to "Under Review", "Approved", or "Rejected". Based on the state, we have different behaviors. If the state is "Received", we need to validate the application details. If the state is "Under Review", we need to assign the application to an underwriter. If the state is "Approved", we need to send an approval letter to the applicant. If the state is "Rejected", we need to send a rejection letter.

We can model each of these states as a separate object that implements a common interface, say LoanApplicationState. This interface will define methods for each of the behavior that is specific to each state. We can also define a Context object that will manage the current state and provide access to the behavior methods.

Here is an example Java code to illustrate this approach:

```java
interface LoanApplicationState {
    void validate(LoanApplication application);
    void assign(LoanApplication application);
    void sendApprovalLetter(LoanApplication application);
    void sendRejectionLetter(LoanApplication application);
}

class ReceivedState implements LoanApplicationState {
    void validate(LoanApplication application) {
        // Perform validation
        application.setState(new UnderReviewState());
    }
    void assign(LoanApplication application) {
        throw new IllegalStateException("Cannot assign until the
            application is under review");
    }
    void sendApprovalLetter(LoanApplication application) {
        throw new IllegalStateException("Cannot send approval until the
             application is approved");
    }
    void sendRejectionLetter(LoanApplication application) {
        throw new IllegalStateException("Cannot send rejection until
            the application is rejected");
    }
}

class UnderReviewState implements LoanApplicationState {
    void validate(LoanApplication application) {
```

```
      // Perform validation
   }
   void assign(LoanApplication application) {
      // Assign to an underwriter
      application.setState(new AssignedState());
   }
   void sendApprovalLetter(LoanApplication application) {
      throw new IllegalStateException("Cannot send approval until the
         application is approved");
   }
   void sendRejectionLetter(LoanApplication application) {
      throw new IllegalStateException("Cannot send rejection until
         the application is rejected");
   }
}

class AssignedState implements LoanApplicationState {
   void validate(LoanApplication application) {
      // Perform validation
   }
   void assign(LoanApplication application) {
      throw new IllegalStateException("Application already assigned")
         ;
   }
   void sendApprovalLetter(LoanApplication application) {
      // Send approval letter to the applicant
      application.setState(new ApprovedState());
   }
   void sendRejectionLetter(LoanApplication application) {
      // Send rejection letter to the applicant
      application.setState(new RejectedState());
   }
}

class ApprovedState implements LoanApplicationState {
   void validate(LoanApplication application) {
      throw new IllegalStateException("Application already approved")
         ;
   }
   void assign(LoanApplication application) {
      throw new IllegalStateException("Cannot assign once application
         is approved");
   }
   void sendApprovalLetter(LoanApplication application) {
      throw new IllegalStateException("Approval letter already sent")
         ;
   }
   void sendRejectionLetter(LoanApplication application) {
      throw new IllegalStateException("Cannot send rejection once
         application is approved");
   }
}
```

```
class RejectedState implements LoanApplicationState {
  void validate(LoanApplication application) {
    throw new IllegalStateException("Cannot validate once
      application is rejected");
  }
  void assign(LoanApplication application) {
    throw new IllegalStateException("Cannot assign once application
      is rejected");
  }
  void sendApprovalLetter(LoanApplication application) {
    throw new IllegalStateException("Cannot send approval once
      application is rejected");
  }
  void sendRejectionLetter(LoanApplication application) {
    throw new IllegalStateException("Rejection letter already sent"
      );
  }
}
class LoanApplication {
  private LoanApplicationState state;

  public LoanApplication() {
    state = new ReceivedState();
  }

  public void setState(LoanApplicationState state) {
    this.state = state;
  }

  public void validate() {
    state.validate(this);
  }

  public void assign() {
    state.assign(this);
  }

  public void sendApprovalLetter() {
    state.sendApprovalLetter(this);
  }

  public void sendRejectionLetter() {
    state.sendRejectionLetter(this);
  }
}
```

In this example, the LoanApplication class represents our Context object. The state is initially set to ReceivedState. We can then call the methods validate, assign, sendApprovalLetter, and sendRejectionLetter on the LoanApplication object. The object will delegate the call to the current state object, which will perform the necessary behavior based on the current state and may change the state of the context object.

In conclusion, the State pattern is an excellent approach for modeling complex workflows and managing stateful microservices by decoupling state management from the business logic, making it easier to maintain and extend.

6.7   Discuss the impact of the Adapter pattern on system architecture when dealing with legacy systems, third-party libraries, or incompatible interfaces at a large scale.

The Adapter pattern is a design pattern that allows the interface of an existing class to be used as another interface. It is often used when integrating new components into an existing system where the new components use a different interface from the rest of the system. The primary goal of the Adapter pattern is to make it easier to reuse existing code within a new system.

When dealing with legacy systems, third-party libraries, or incompatible interfaces at a large scale, the Adapter pattern can have a significant impact on system architecture in a few different ways:

1. Flexibility: The Adapter pattern provides flexibility by allowing new components with incompatible interfaces to be integrated into an existing system. This increases the agility of

the system as a whole, making it easier to respond to changing
business requirements. In addition, it allows organizations to
take advantage of the latest technology even if it does not fully
integrate with existing components.

2. Complexity: Using the Adapter pattern adds an additional
layer of complexity to the system architecture. This is because
the Adapter must translate between two different interfaces,
which adds computational overhead. Additionally, there may
be multiple Adapters required to translate between all of the
different interfaces that need to be integrated.

3. Maintenance: The Adapter pattern can make maintenance
more complex because there may be multiple Adapters that
need to be maintained in order to keep the system up-to-date.
This can add to the overall cost of ownership of the system.

To illustrate the impact of the Adapter pattern on system architecture, consider a scenario where a company has a legacy
system that uses a proprietary database. The company wants
to integrate a new third-party analytics platform into the system that requires data to be stored in a different database.
Because the two databases have incompatible interfaces, an
Adapter must be created to translate between them.

Here is an example implementation of the Adapter pattern in
Java:

```java
public interface LegacyDatabase {
   void saveData(String data);
}

public class ProprietaryDatabase implements LegacyDatabase {
   public void saveData(String data) {
      // proprietary implementation
   }
}
```

```
public interface NewDatabase {
   void storeData(String data);
}

public class ThirdPartyDatabase implements NewDatabase {
   public void storeData(String data) {
      // third-party implementation
   }
}

public class DatabaseAdapter implements NewDatabase {
   private LegacyDatabase legacyDatabase;

   public DatabaseAdapter(LegacyDatabase legacyDatabase) {
      this.legacyDatabase = legacyDatabase;
   }

   public void storeData(String data) {
      legacyDatabase.saveData(data);
   }
}
```

In this example, the ProprietaryDatabase class represents the existing legacy database and the ThirdPartyDatabase class represents the new database required by the analytics platform. The DatabaseAdapter class acts as a bridge between the two databases by implementing the NewDatabase interface and delegating the implementation to the LegacyDatabase implementation through composition.

In conclusion, the Adapter pattern can have a significant impact on system architecture when integrating new components into an existing system with incompatible interfaces. It provides flexibility by allowing the integration of new technology into legacy systems, but adds complexity and maintenance overhead to the overall system architecture.

6.8   Analyze the role of the Command pattern in implementing event sourcing and how it can be used to build fault-tolerant, scalable, and distributed systems.

The Command pattern is a behavioral design pattern that encapsulates a request as an object, thereby letting you parameterize clients with different requests, queue or log requests, and support undoable operations. The Command pattern fits well with event sourcing, an architectural pattern for complex systems where every change to the system state is captured as a sequence of immutable events. Event sourcing offers several benefits, such as auditability and reproducibility, but it also imposes challenges, such as how to handle concurrency, consistency, and failure.

Using the Command pattern in event sourcing means representing each command that triggers a state change as an event. A command is an intent to perform an action, while an event is a record of something that has happened. The difference is that a command may or may not succeed and may or may not have side effects, while an event is always immutable and always reflects a definite state of the system. By modeling commands as events, we separate concerns between the input (what the user wants) and the output (what the system does), and we make it easy to replay, debug, optimize, or restore the system.

To illustrate how the Command pattern can be used for event sourcing, let's consider an example of a shopping cart system. Suppose that we want to implement a feature where a user can add, remove, or update items in their shopping cart, and the

cart is stored in a distributed database that supports ACID
transactions. We can define the following classes:

```
// A command to add an item to the cart
class AddItemCommand implements Command {
  private final String cartId;
  private final String itemId;
  private final int quantity;
  public AddItemCommand(String cartId, String itemId, int quantity)
      {
    this.cartId = cartId;
    this.itemId = itemId;
    this.quantity = quantity;
  }
  public void execute() {
    ShoppingCart cart = ShoppingCartRepository.findById(cartId);
    cart.addItem(itemId, quantity);
    ShoppingCartRepository.save(cart);
    EventBus.publish(new ItemAddedToCartEvent(cartId, itemId,
        quantity));
  }
}

// A command to remove an item from the cart
class RemoveItemCommand implements Command {
  private final String cartId;
  private final String itemId;
  public RemoveItemCommand(String cartId, String itemId) {
    this.cartId = cartId;
    this.itemId = itemId;
  }
  public void execute() {
    ShoppingCart cart = ShoppingCartRepository.findById(cartId);
    cart.removeItem(itemId);
    ShoppingCartRepository.save(cart);
    EventBus.publish(new ItemRemovedFromCartEvent(cartId, itemId));
  }
}

// A command to update the quantity of an item in the cart
class UpdateItemCommand implements Command {
  private final String cartId;
  private final String itemId;
  private final int quantity;
  public UpdateItemCommand(String cartId, String itemId, int
      quantity) {
    this.cartId = cartId;
    this.itemId = itemId;
    this.quantity = quantity;
  }
  public void execute() {
    ShoppingCart cart = ShoppingCartRepository.findById(cartId);
    cart.updateItem(itemId, quantity);
    ShoppingCartRepository.save(cart);
```

```
    EventBus.publish(new ItemUpdatedInCartEvent(cartId, itemId,
        quantity));
  }
}

// An event that represents an item added to a cart
class ItemAddedToCartEvent implements Event {
  private final String cartId;
  private final String itemId;
  private final int quantity;
  public ItemAddedToCartEvent(String cartId, String itemId, int
      quantity) {
    this.cartId = cartId;
    this.itemId = itemId;
    this.quantity = quantity;
  }
  public void apply() {
    ShoppingCart cart = ShoppingCartRepository.findById(cartId);
    cart.addItem(itemId, quantity);
    ShoppingCartRepository.save(cart);
  }
}

// An event that represents an item removed from a cart
class ItemRemovedFromCartEvent implements Event {
  private final String cartId;
  private final String itemId;
  public ItemRemovedFromCartEvent(String cartId, String itemId) {
    this.cartId = cartId;
    this.itemId = itemId;
  }
  public void apply() {
    ShoppingCart cart = ShoppingCartRepository.findById(cartId);
    cart.removeItem(itemId);
    ShoppingCartRepository.save(cart);
  }
}

// An event that represents an item updated in a cart
class ItemUpdatedInCartEvent implements Event {
  private final String cartId;
  private final String itemId;
  private final int quantity;
  public ItemUpdatedInCartEvent(String cartId, String itemId, int
      quantity) {
    this.cartId = cartId;
    this.itemId = itemId;
    this.quantity = quantity;
  }
  public void apply() {
    ShoppingCart cart = ShoppingCartRepository.findById(cartId);
    cart.updateItem(itemId, quantity);
    ShoppingCartRepository.save(cart);
  }
}
```

In this example, each command implements the Command interface, which has a single method 'execute()'. The execute method fetches the current state of the shopping cart using a repository, invokes a method on the cart that performs the requested action (add, remove, or update), saves the cart to the repository, and publishes an event that corresponds to the action. The event also implements the Event interface, which has a single method 'apply()'. The apply method fetches the current state of the shopping cart using a repository, invokes a method that updates the cart to reflect the event, and saves the cart to the repository. The EventBus class is responsible for subscribing to events and dispatching them to listeners that are interested in handling them.

One advantage of using the Command pattern in event sourcing is that it makes it easy to implement fault tolerance. When a command fails to execute, it can be retried, logged, or forwarded to a fallback system. Similarly, when an event fails to apply, it can be retried, logged, or discarded. By separating the execution of a command from its result, we decouple the command processing from the system state and allow for more flexible error handling.

Another advantage of using the Command pattern in event sourcing is that it makes it easy to implement scalability and distribution. Because each command and event is a self-contained unit of work, it can be processed independently by different nodes in a cluster or in a message queue. The nodes do not need to know about each other's state or behavior, as long as they share the same Command and Event interfaces. By using message brokers or event-based architectures, we can achieve high availability, low latency, and high throughput for the system.

In conclusion, the Command pattern is a useful tool for implementing event sourcing, as it provides a clear separation between commands and events, and it enables fault tolerance, scalability, and distribution. By using the Command pattern, we can ensure that every change to the system state is captured as a sequence of immutable events, and that every action that triggers a state change is represented as a command. This makes it possible to build complex systems that are transparent, auditable, and robust.

6.9 Discuss the impact of the Prototype pattern on memory management, garbage collection, and performance optimization in large-scale applications with frequent object creation.

The Prototype pattern is a creational design pattern that supports the dynamic creation of objects by cloning an existing object. It is particularly useful when creating new objects is expensive, and the majority of the state of the objects remains constant across all instances.

In large-scale applications that frequently create new objects, the Prototype pattern can have a significant impact on memory management, garbage collection, and performance optimization.

Memory Management:

When objects are frequently created, memory management becomes critical. In Java, objects are created on the heap and are managed by a garbage collector that periodically frees unused memory. Frequent object creation can cause heap fragmentation, making it difficult for the garbage collector to free unused memory. The Prototype pattern can help manage memory by reducing the number of objects that need to be created. Instead of creating entirely new objects, the Prototype pattern clones an existing object and modifies only the necessary attributes.

Garbage Collection:

Garbage collection in Java is a non-deterministic process, which means that the Java Virtual Machine (JVM) governs it. Frequent object creation can lead to high pressure on the garbage collector, which can result in long pauses, decreased application responsiveness, and even out of memory errors. The Prototype pattern can ease this pressure by reducing the number of new objects created, thus resulting in fewer objects to be cleaned up by the garbage collector.

Performance Optimization:

Frequent object creation can have a severe impact on the application's performance, especially if the object creation process is expensive. Expensive object creation can involve I/O operations, database queries, or heavy computation, which can have a significant impact on the application's performance. The Prototype pattern helps optimize performance by reducing the number of new objects that are created. By cloning an existing object instead of creating a new one, we can reduce the cost of object creation, which often leads to improved application performance.

Here is an example of how the Prototype pattern can be implemented in Java:

```java
public abstract class Shape implements Cloneable {
    private String id;
    protected String type;

    public String getType(){
        return type;
    }

    public String getId() {
        return id;
    }

    public void setId(String id) {
        this.id = id;
    }

    public abstract void draw();

    public Object clone() {
        Object clone = null;

        try {
            clone = super.clone();

        } catch (CloneNotSupportedException e) {
            e.printStackTrace();
        }

        return clone;
    }
}

public class Circle extends Shape {

    public Circle(){
        type = "Circle";
    }

    @Override
    public void draw() {
        System.out.println("Inside Circle::draw() method.");
    }
}

public class Square extends Shape {

    public Square(){
        type = "Square";
    }

    @Override
    public void draw() {
        System.out.println("Inside Square::draw() method.");
    }
}
```

```
public class ShapeCache {
    private static Map<String, Shape> shapeMap = new HashMap<String,
        Shape>();

    public static Shape getShape(String shapeId) {
        Shape cachedShape = shapeMap.get(shapeId);
        return (Shape) cachedShape.clone();
    }

    public static void loadCache() {
        Circle circle = new Circle();
        circle.setId("1");
        shapeMap.put(circle.getId(),circle);

        Square square = new Square();
        square.setId("2");
        shapeMap.put(square.getId(),square);
    }
}

public class PrototypeTest {
    public static void main(String[] args) {
        ShapeCache.loadCache();

        Shape clonedShape = (Shape) ShapeCache.getShape("1");
        System.out.println("Shape␣:␣" + clonedShape.getType());

        Shape clonedShape2 = (Shape) ShapeCache.getShape("2");
        System.out.println("Shape␣:␣" + clonedShape2.getType());
    }
}
```

In this example, the ShapeCache class demonstrates the Prototype pattern by loading predefined shapes into the shapeMap.
Whenever a shape is requested, the ShapeCache clones the prototype object rather than creating a new shape, reducing the
number of objects created, and easing the load on memory management and garbage collection. Cloning the object also saves
any expensive operation that shape creation may require, leading to performance optimization.

6.10   Explain how the Builder pattern can be adapted to support advanced object creation scenarios, such as object pooling, lazy initialization, or object recycling.

The Builder pattern is a creational software design pattern that allows us to create objects by providing flexible steps to initialize them, without compromising on immutability. The basic idea behind the Builder design pattern is to separate the construction of objects from their representation. This separation optimizes the design, structuring, and testing of an object-oriented software system.

The basic version of the Builder pattern provides a set of methods which can be used to configure and construct a complex object with multiple optional components. But in advanced object creation scenarios, there could be additional requirements, such as object pooling, lazy initialization, and object recycling, to optimize resource usage and performance.

To support such scenarios, the Builder pattern can be adapted as follows:

Object Pooling Scenario

Object pooling is a technique of reusing objects that have already been created, instead of creating new objects every time they are needed, thus reducing the burden of object creation and destruction. When using the builder pattern to create objects in this scenario, the builder would need to keep track of the objects that have already been created and reuse them where possible.

Here's an example implementation of the builder pattern that supports object pooling:

```
public class Resource {
    // code for the resource class
}

public interface ResourceBuilder {
    public Resource build();
}

public class PooledResourceBuilder implements ResourceBuilder {
    private Resource resource;

    public PooledResourceBuilder() {
        // initialize the pool of objects
    }

    @Override
    public Resource build() {
        if (resource is available in pool) {
            return resource;
        } else {
            // create a new object and add it to the pool
            resource = new Resource();
            add resource to pool;
            return resource;
        }
    }
}
```

Lazy Initialization Scenario

Lazy initialization is a technique of initializing objects only when they are actually needed, thus delaying their creation until that point. When using the builder pattern to create objects in this scenario, the builder would only initialize the object properties when they are first accessed.

Here's an example implementation of the builder pattern that supports lazy initialization:

```
public class Resource {
    // code for the resource class
```

```
}
public interface ResourceBuilder {
    public void setProperty1(Property1 property1);
    public void setProperty2(Property2 property2);
    // more properties to be set
    public Resource build();
}

public class LazyResourceBuilder implements ResourceBuilder {
    private Property1 property1;
    private Property2 property2;
    // more properties

    @Override
    public void setProperty1(Property1 property1) {
        this.property1 = property1;
    }

    @Override
    public void setProperty2(Property2 property2) {
        this.property2 = property2;
    }

    // more setters

    @Override
    public Resource build() {
        Resource resource = new Resource();
        resource.setProperty1(this.property1);
        resource.setProperty2(this.property2);
        // set more properties
        return resource;
    }
}
```

Object Recycling Scenario

Object recycling is a technique of reusing objects that were
previously used and released, rather than creating new objects.
When using the builder pattern to create objects in this scenario, the builder would not destroy the object when it is released, but keep it in a pool and reuse it when possible.

Here's an example implementation of the builder pattern that
supports object recycling:

```
public class Resource {
```

```
    // code for the resource class
}

public interface ResourceBuilder {
    public void setProperty1(Property1 property1);
    public void setProperty2(Property2 property2);
    // more properties to be set
    public Resource build();
    public void release(Resource resource);
}

public class RecyclableResourceBuilder implements ResourceBuilder {
    private Map<UUID, Resource> pool;
    private Property1 property1;
    private Property2 property2;
    // more properties

    public RecyclableResourceBuilder() {
        // initialize the pool of objects
    }

    @Override
    public void setProperty1(Property1 property1) {
        this.property1 = property1;
    }

    @Override
    public void setProperty2(Property2 property2) {
        this.property2 = property2;
    }

    // more setters

    @Override
    public Resource build() {
        if (pool is not empty) {
            // reuse a previous object
            Resource resource = pool.remove(0);
            resource.setProperty1(this.property1);
            resource.setProperty2(this.property2);
            // set more properties
            return resource;
        } else {
            // create a new object
            Resource resource = new Resource();
            resource.setProperty1(this.property1);
            resource.setProperty2(this.property2);
            // set more properties
            return resource;
        }
    }

    @Override
    public void release(Resource resource) {
        // reset the properties and add the object to the pool
```

```
            resource.reset();
            pool.add(resource);
        }
    }
```

In summary, the Builder pattern can be adapted to support advanced object creation scenarios by adding additional logic to reuse and recycle objects, along with their properties, to optimize resource usage and performance.

6.11   Discuss the implications of using the Facade pattern in API Gateway design, taking into account aspects such as caching, rate limiting, and security.

The Facade pattern is often used in API Gateway design, as it simplifies the interaction between clients and multiple back-end services by providing a single entry point. When using the Facade pattern in API Gateway design, it is important to consider the implications it has on caching, rate limiting, and security.

Caching:

Caching is an important performance optimization technique that reduces the response time for frequently requested data. In API Gateway design, caching is typically implemented at the gateway level to prevent requests from reaching the back-end services unnecessarily. When using the Facade pattern, it is important to ensure that caching is applied consistently across all back-end services and that the gateway itself doesn't cache data in a way that can lead to inconsistencies. The Facade pattern also provides an opportunity for caching at the gateway level, where responses can be cached based on common requests that are shared across multiple back-end services.

Rate Limiting:

Rate limiting is another important aspect of API Gateway design that prevents clients from flooding the back-end services with requests. When using the Facade pattern, rate limiting can be applied consistently across all back-end services by configuring the gateway to monitor and limit the requests that are being made. By doing so, the Facade pattern provides an opportunity to prevent unauthorized access, limit usage, and ensure that back-end services are not overwhelmed.

Security:

Security is an essential consideration in API Gateway design, as the gateway is the first line of defense against unauthorized access to back-end services. When using the Facade pattern, security can be applied consistently across all back-end services by implementing a set of security policies that are enforced at the gateway level. This includes authentication, authorization, and encryption policies that can be enforced across all back-end services to prevent unauthorized access and ensure that sensitive data is protected.

Java Example:

```
public class ApiGateway {
    private final AuthenticationService authenticationService;
    private final AuthorizationService authorizationService;
    private final EncryptionService encryptionService;
    private final RateLimiter rateLimiter;
```

```
public ApiGateway(AuthenticationService authenticationService,
                  AuthorizationService authorizationService,
                  EncryptionService encryptionService,
                  RateLimiter rateLimiter) {
    this.authenticationService = authenticationService;
    this.authorizationService = authorizationService;
    this.encryptionService = encryptionService;
    this.rateLimiter = rateLimiter;
}

public ApiResponse processRequest(ApiRequest request) {
    // Apply rate limiting
    if (rateLimiter.isRequestAllowed(request)) {
        // Apply authentication
        if (authenticationService.authenticate(request)) {
            // Apply authorization
            if (authorizationService.authorize(request)) {
                // Apply encryption
                return encryptionService.encrypt(request.process())
                    ;
            } else {
                throw new AuthorizationException("Unauthorized␣
                    access");
            }
        } else {
            throw new AuthenticationException("Invalid␣credentials
                ");
        }
    } else {
        throw new RateLimitException("Too␣many␣requests");
    }
}
}
```

6.12 Analyze the role of the Chain of Responsibility pattern in implementing distributed and fault-tolerant request processing pipelines in large-scale systems.

The Chain of Responsibility pattern is designed to create a pipeline of handlers for handling a request. This pattern is highly useful in large-scale systems where there are multiple processing stages and the processing of a request is dependent on the state of the system. In such systems, it is important to have a distributed and fault-tolerant approach for request processing, and the Chain of Responsibility pattern plays a crucial role in achieving this.

Distributed Request Processing: In a large-scale system, request processing is often distributed across multiple nodes to handle the volume of requests efficiently. The Chain of Responsibility pattern can be used to create a pipeline of handlers across these nodes to process requests asynchronously. Each node in the pipeline can be responsible for a specific stage of processing, and the request can be passed from one node to the next until it is processed completely. This approach helps in achieving scalability and reducing the load on any single node.

Fault-Tolerant Request Processing: In a distributed system, it is important to handle failures gracefully. The Chain of Responsibility pattern can be used to achieve fault tolerance by introducing redundancy in the processing pipeline. Multiple handlers can be added for each stage of processing, and the request can be processed by any available handler. This approach helps in ensuring that the processing of a request is not affected by the failure of any single node.

Let us consider an example of distributed and fault-tolerant request processing using the Chain of Responsibility pattern. Suppose we have a system that processes customer orders. The order processing involves multiple stages, such as validation, pricing, inventory check, and payment processing. We can create a pipeline of handlers for each stage of processing as follows:

```
public interface OrderHandler {
    void process(Order order);
```

```
    void setNextHandler(OrderHandler nextHandler);
}

public class ValidationHandler implements OrderHandler {
    private OrderHandler nextHandler;

    @Override
    public void process(Order order) {
        // Validate the order
        if (isValid(order)) {
            nextHandler.process(order);
        } else {
            // Handle invalid order
        }
    }

    @Override
    public void setNextHandler(OrderHandler nextHandler) {
        this.nextHandler = nextHandler;
    }

    private boolean isValid(Order order) {
        // Check if the order is valid
    }
}

// Similar handler classes for pricing, inventory check, and payment
    processing

public class OrderProcessor {
    private List<OrderHandler> handlers;

    public void process(Order order) {
        // Start processing the order
        handlers.get(0).process(order);
    }

    public void setHandlers(List<OrderHandler> handlers) {
        // Build the processing pipeline
        for (int i = 0; i < handlers.size() - 1; i++) {
            handlers.get(i).setNextHandler(handlers.get(i + 1));
        }
        this.handlers = handlers;
    }
}
```

In the above example, the OrderProcessor class represents the
entry point for the processing pipeline. The setHandlers() method
is used to set up the processing pipeline by adding the handlers
for each stage of processing. The process() method of the OrderProcessor class starts processing the order by passing it to

the first handler in the pipeline (i.e., the ValidationHandler).

Now, let's assume that we have distributed the order processing across multiple nodes to achieve scalability. We can deploy each handler in a separate node and connect them using a messaging system (such as Apache Kafka or RabbitMQ). Each node can process the order asynchronously and pass it to the next node in the pipeline using the messaging system.

To achieve fault tolerance, we can introduce redundancy in the processing pipeline by deploying multiple instances of each handler. Each instance can process the order independently, and the messaging system can ensure that the order is processed by any available instance of each handler.

In conclusion, the Chain of Responsibility pattern is highly useful in implementing distributed and fault-tolerant request processing pipelines in large-scale systems. This pattern helps achieve scalability, fault tolerance, and modularity in the processing pipeline.

6.13 Explain how the Composite pattern can be combined with other structural patterns like the Proxy, Bridge, or Flyweight patterns to address complex architectural challenges.

The Composite pattern is a structural pattern that allows clients to treat individual objects and compositions of objects uniformly. It composes objects into tree structures and allows clients to work with these structures in a recursive manner,

as if the objects were individual entities. On the other hand,
Proxy, Bridge, and Flyweight patterns are also structural patterns that provide solutions to different architectural challenges.
In this answer, I will discuss how the Composite pattern can be
combined with each of these patterns.

1. Composite and Proxy pattern:

The Composite pattern can be combined with the Proxy pattern to protect access to the components of a composite structure. The Proxy pattern provides a surrogate or placeholder
for another object in order to control access to it. By using a
proxy, a client can control access to the components of a composite structure, allowing or denying access whenever needed.
The composite structure can be seen as the real subject, while
the proxy provides a level of indirection to access its components.

Example code in Java:

```java
public interface Component {
  void operation();
}

public class Leaf implements Component {
  @Override
  public void operation() {
    // leaf operation logic
  }
}

public class Composite implements Component {
  private List<Component> components = new ArrayList<>();

  public void add(Component component) {
    components.add(component);
  }

  public void remove(Component component) {
    components.remove(component);
  }

  @Override
```

```
    public void operation() {
      for (Component component : components) {
        component.operation();
      }
    }
}
public class Proxy implements Component {
  private Component component;

  public Proxy(Component component) {
    this.component = component;
  }

  @Override
  public void operation() {
    // access control logic here
    component.operation();
  }
}
```

2. Composite and Bridge pattern:

The Composite pattern can be combined with the Bridge pattern to decouple abstractions from their implementations. The Bridge pattern provides a mechanism to decouple an abstraction from its implementation, allowing both to vary independently. By using the Bridge pattern together with the Composite pattern, a client can create complex structures consisting of abstractions and their implementations, without exposing the implementation details to the client.

Example code in Java:

```
public interface Abstraction {
  void operation();
}
public class RefinedAbstraction implements Abstraction {
  private Implementor implementor;

  public RefinedAbstraction(Implementor implementor) {
    this.implementor = implementor;
  }

  @Override
  public void operation() {
```

```
      implementor.operationImpl();
   }
}

public interface Implementor {
   void operationImpl();
}

public class ConcreteImplementor implements Implementor {
   @Override
   public void operationImpl() {
      // implementation logic here
   }
}

public abstract class Composite implements Abstraction {
   private List<Abstraction> abstractions = new ArrayList<>();

   public void add(Abstraction abstraction) {
      abstractions.add(abstraction);
   }

   public void remove(Abstraction abstraction) {
      abstractions.remove(abstraction);
   }

   @Override
   public void operation() {
      for (Abstraction abstraction : abstractions) {
         abstraction.operation();
      }
   }
}

public class Leaf extends RefinedAbstraction {
   public Leaf(Implementor implementor) {
      super(implementor);
   }
}
```

3. Composite and Flyweight pattern:

The Composite pattern can be combined with the Flyweight
pattern to share common parts of a composite structure. The
Flyweight pattern provides a mechanism to share objects that
have similar or identical state, reducing memory usage and improving performance. By using the Flyweight pattern together
with the Composite pattern, a client can create complex struc-

tures consisting of both shared and non-shared parts, reducing
the memory usage and improving the performance of the system.

Example code in Java:

```java
public interface Component {
    void operation();
}

public class ConcreteComponent implements Component {
    private String intrinsicState;

    public ConcreteComponent(String intrinsicState) {
        this.intrinsicState = intrinsicState;
    }

    @Override
    public void operation() {
        // operation logic here
    }
}

public class FlyweightFactory {
    private Map<String, Component> flyweights = new HashMap<>();

    public Component getFlyweight(String intrinsicState) {
        if (!flyweights.containsKey(intrinsicState)) {
            flyweights.put(intrinsicState, new ConcreteComponent(
                intrinsicState));
        }
        return flyweights.get(intrinsicState);
    }
}

public abstract class Composite implements Component {
    private List<Component> components = new ArrayList<>();

    public void add(Component component) {
        components.add(component);
    }

    public void remove(Component component) {
        components.remove(component);
    }

    @Override
    public void operation() {
        for (Component component : components) {
            component.operation();
        }
    }
```

```
}

public class Client {
  private FlyweightFactory factory;

  public Client(FlyweightFactory factory) {
    this.factory = factory;
  }

  public void createComposite() {
    Composite composite = new Composite();
    Component flyweight = factory.getFlyweight("shared␣state");
    composite.add(flyweight);
    composite.add(new ConcreteComponent("non-shared␣state"));
  }
}
```

In summary, the Composite pattern can be combined with other structural patterns to address complex architectural challenges, such as access control, decoupling of abstractions and implementations, and efficient use of resources. The combined use of these patterns can provide more flexible and efficient solutions to complex design problems.

6.14   Discuss the impact of the Flyweight pattern on system design and resource management in large-scale applications with shared resources and high concurrency.

The Flyweight design pattern is particularly useful in large-scale applications with shared resources and high concurrency because it reduces the memory footprint of objects by sharing intrinsic data across multiple instances. This can lead to significant savings in terms of required memory, especially when dealing with large sets of similar objects.

The central idea of the Flyweight pattern is to separate an object's intrinsic state from its extrinsic state. The intrinsic state is the part of the object that can be shared across multiple instances, while the extrinsic state is the part that varies from one instance to another. By sharing the intrinsic state, the pattern ensures that redundant memory allocations are avoided, leading to a reduction in memory usage.

In addition to reducing memory usage, the Flyweight pattern can also improve the performance of the application by reducing the number of objects that need to be created and managed. In large-scale applications with high concurrency, the creation of objects can become a bottleneck, especially if the objects are heavyweight and require significant amounts of memory to be allocated. By using the Flyweight pattern to share objects, the application can avoid the overhead of object creation, leading to faster performance and better scalability.

To illustrate the impact of the Flyweight pattern on system design and resource management, consider a hypothetical example of a graphics rendering application that needs to render large numbers of identical objects, such as trees or rocks, in a scene. Without the Flyweight pattern, the application would need to create a separate object for each instance of the object, leading to a large memory footprint and potentially significant performance overhead due to object creation.

With the Flyweight pattern, the application can create a single shared object that contains the intrinsic state of the object, such as its shape, color, and texture, and that can be reused across multiple instances. Each instance of the object then only needs to store its own extrinsic state, such as its position and orientation, leading to a significant reduction in memory usage.

Java code example of using Flyweight pattern:

```java
public interface Tree {
   public void draw(int x, int y);
}

public class TreeType implements Tree {
   private String name;
   private String color;
   private String texture;

   public TreeType(String name, String color, String texture) {
      this.name = name;
      this.color = color;
      this.texture = texture;
   }

   public void draw(int x, int y) {
      System.out.println("Drawing " + name + " tree at (" + x + "," +
         y + ")");
   }
}

public class TreeFactory {
   private static Map<String, TreeType> treeTypes = new HashMap<
      String, TreeType>();

   public static TreeType getTreeType(String name, String color,
      String texture) {
      TreeType treeType = treeTypes.get(name);

      if (treeType == null) {
         treeType = new TreeType(name, color, texture);
         treeTypes.put(name, treeType);
      }

      return treeType;
   }
}

public class TreeRenderer {
   public void renderTree(String name, int x, int y) {
      TreeType treeType = TreeFactory.getTreeType(name, "green", "
         smooth");
      treeType.draw(x, y);
   }
}
```

In this example, we have a 'TreeType' interface that defines the 'draw()' method for drawing a tree at a given position. We then have a concrete implementation of 'TreeType' that stores the intrinsic state of the tree, such as its name, color, and texture.

To share 'TreeType' objects and avoid redundant memory allocations, we use a 'TreeFactory' class that maintains a cache of 'TreeType' objects based on their names. Whenever a new 'TreeType' object needs to be created, the 'TreeFactory' first checks if an object with the same name already exists in the cache. If so, it returns the shared object; otherwise, it creates a new object and adds it to the cache.

Finally, we have a 'TreeRenderer' class that uses the 'TreeFactory' to get a 'TreeType' object and then calls its 'draw()' method to render the tree at the given position.

With this setup, we can create and reuse 'TreeType' objects as needed, avoiding the overhead of creating and managing redundant objects. This can lead to significant efficiencies in terms of memory usage and performance, especially in large-scale applications with high concurrency.

6.15 Analyze the role of the Mediator pattern in implementing complex coordination and orchestration tasks in distributed systems, such as service mesh or workflow engines.

The Mediator pattern is a behavioral pattern that promotes loose coupling between objects by encapsulating the interactions among them. In a distributed system, where there are multiple components running on different nodes, coordination and orchestration tasks can become complex and challenging to manage. The Mediator pattern can help alleviate these challenges by providing a centralized component that facilitates communication and collaboration among the different components.

In a service mesh architecture, the Mediator pattern can be used to implement a control plane that manages the behavior of the network of services. The control plane acts as a mediator between the services, handling tasks such as service discovery, load balancing, and traffic management. For example, in Istio, the service mesh platform, the Istio Pilot component acts as a mediator between the services, managing traffic routing and configuring the Envoy proxies that are deployed alongside the services.

Similarly, in a workflow engine, the Mediator pattern can be used to coordinate the activities of the different workflow components. The workflow engine acts as a mediator between the workflow tasks, handling tasks such as task scheduling, error handling, and data management. For example, the Apache Airflow workflow engine provides a DAG (Directed Acyclic Graph) scheduler that acts as a mediator between the tasks in the workflow, managing the dependencies between them and executing them in the correct order.

Java Code Example:

```java
public interface Mediator {
    void send(String message, Component sender);
}

public abstract class Component {
    private Mediator mediator;

    public Component(Mediator mediator) {
        this.mediator = mediator;
    }

    public void send(String message) {
```

```
      mediator.send(message, this);
  }

  public abstract void receive(String message);
}

public class ConcreteComponent extends Component {
  public ConcreteComponent(Mediator mediator) {
    super(mediator);
  }

  public void receive(String message) {
    System.out.println("Received message: " + message);
  }
}

public class ConcreteMediator implements Mediator {
  private ConcreteComponent component1;
  private ConcreteComponent component2;

  public void setComponent1(ConcreteComponent component1) {
    this.component1 = component1;
  }

  public void setComponent2(ConcreteComponent component2) {
    this.component2 = component2;
  }

  public void send(String message, Component sender) {
    if (sender.equals(component1)) {
      component2.receive(message);
    } else {
      component1.receive(message);
    }
  }
}
```

In this example, we have a Mediator interface and a Component
abstract class that define the Mediator pattern. ConcreteComponent and ConcreteMediator are concrete implementations of
the Mediator pattern. The ConcreteMediator acts as a mediator between two ConcreteComponents, executing the send()
method when a component sends a message. The Concrete-
Component receives messages via its receive() method. This
shows how the Mediator pattern can be used to manage communication among distributed components in a system.

6.16   Discuss the implications of using the Proxy pattern for caching, load balancing, or security in large-scale and distributed systems.

The Proxy pattern is a popular design pattern used for various architectural purposes in large-scale and distributed systems, such as caching, load balancing, and security. In this answer, we will discuss the implications of using the Proxy pattern for each of these purposes.

Caching:

Caching is a commonly used technique to improve the performance of a system by storing frequently accessed data in memory or in a dedicated cache. In distributed systems, caching can be achieved using a proxy server that intercepts requests and caches responses for future use. The proxy server acts as an intermediary between clients and servers, and can improve response time and reduce network traffic. The Proxy pattern can be used to implement such a proxy server, providing a simple and extensible mechanism for caching.

For example, consider a web application that displays stock prices. Instead of fetching stock prices from a remote server every time a user requests them, a proxy server can be used to cache the prices and reduce the load on the remote server. The Proxy pattern can be used to implement this caching mechanism, with the proxy server intercepting requests and checking if the requested data is available in the cache. If the data is available, it is returned immediately, otherwise the proxy server fetches it from the remote server and caches it for future requests.

Load Balancing:

Load balancing is another commonly used technique in distributed systems that involves distributing incoming network traffic across multiple servers to improve performance and reliability. A proxy server can be used to implement load balancing by distributing requests across multiple backend servers, based on various algorithms such as round-robin, random, or weighted round-robin. The Proxy pattern can be used to implement such a proxy server, providing a simple and flexible mechanism for load balancing.

For example, consider a web application that handles a large volume of incoming requests. By using a load balancing proxy server, the incoming requests can be distributed across multiple backend servers, improving performance and allowing the system to handle more requests. The Proxy pattern can be used to implement this load balancing mechanism, with the proxy server intercepting requests and forwarding them to backend servers based on a load balancing algorithm.

Security:

Security is an important concern in distributed systems, and a proxy server can be used to implement various security-related mechanisms, such as authentication, authorization, and encryption. The Proxy pattern can be used to implement a security proxy that intercepts requests and ensures that only authorized users are allowed to access the requested resources.

For example, consider a web application that requires users to authenticate before accessing certain resources. By using a security proxy server, the authentication process can be centralized and enforced by the proxy server. The Proxy pattern can be used to implement this security mechanism, with the proxy server intercepting requests and checking if the user is authorized to access the requested resource.

In conclusion, the Proxy pattern is a powerful design pattern that can be used for various architectural purposes in large-scale and distributed systems, such as caching, load balancing, and security. By using the Proxy pattern, developers can implement these mechanisms in a simple, extensible, and flexible way.

6.17   Explain how the Bridge pattern can be used to address challenges related to multiple dimensions of variability and extensibility in complex system architectures.

The Bridge design pattern is a structural pattern that decouples an abstraction from its implementation so that both can vary independently. In other words, it separates an abstract class from its implementation, allowing for changes to be made to each independently without affecting the other. This makes it useful in addressing challenges related to multiple dimensions of variability and extensibility in complex system architectures.

A complex system architecture often involves multiple dimensions of variability, such as different platforms, operating systems, databases or protocols, leading to a large number of classes and interfaces. Additionally, as the system evolves or new requirements arise, it may have to be extended in multiple directions, requiring potentially large-scale changes to the codebase. In such cases, it is important to have a design that can separate these concerns and allow for flexibility and extensibility.

The Bridge pattern consists of two parts: an abstraction and an implementation, which are connected by a bridge. The abstraction defines the interface that the client interacts with, while the implementation defines the actual implementation of that interface. The bridge connects the two by allowing different implementations to be used with the same abstraction.

Let's consider an example. Suppose we have a drawing application that can draw different shapes on different platforms (such as a desktop application, a web application or a mobile application). We can start by defining an abstract Shape class and its implementation classes, each of which is tied to a particular platform. However, this creates a tight coupling between the abstraction and its implementation, making it difficult to add new shapes or platforms without changing the existing code.

By introducing a bridge, we can decouple the Shape abstraction from its implementations. We can define a separate interface for each platform, such as DesktopShape, WebShape and MobileShape, and a separate implementation class for each shape, such as Circle, Square, and Triangle. The Shape abstraction would then reference the platform-specific interface, and the implementation classes would implement this interface. This allows us to add new shapes or platforms without changing the existing code, as long as we provide a new implementation class that adheres to the platform-specific interface.

Here is an example implementation of the Bridge pattern in

Java:

```java
// Abstraction
public abstract class Shape {
    protected ShapeImpl shapeImpl;

    public Shape(ShapeImpl shapeImpl) {
        this.shapeImpl = shapeImpl;
    }

    public abstract void draw();
}

// Implementor
public interface ShapeImpl {
    public void drawCircle();
    public void drawSquare();
    public void drawTriangle();
}

// Concrete Implementors
public class DesktopShapeImpl implements ShapeImpl {
    @Override
    public void drawCircle() {
        // draw circle on desktop
    }

    @Override
    public void drawSquare() {
        // draw square on desktop
    }

    @Override
    public void drawTriangle() {
        // draw triangle on desktop
    }
}

public class WebShapeImpl implements ShapeImpl {
    @Override
    public void drawCircle() {
        // draw circle on web
    }

    @Override
    public void drawSquare() {
        // draw square on web
    }

    @Override
    public void drawTriangle() {
        // draw triangle on web
    }
}
```

```
// Refined Abstractions
public class Circle extends Shape {
    public Circle(ShapeImpl shapeImpl) {
        super(shapeImpl);
    }

    public void draw() {
        shapeImpl.drawCircle();
    }
}

public class Square extends Shape {
    public Square(ShapeImpl shapeImpl) {
        super(shapeImpl);
    }

    public void draw() {
        shapeImpl.drawSquare();
    }
}

public class Triangle extends Shape {
    public Triangle(ShapeImpl shapeImpl) {
        super(shapeImpl);
    }

    public void draw() {
        shapeImpl.drawTriangle();
    }
}

// Client
public class Client {
    public static void main(String[] args) {
        Shape desktopCircle = new Circle(new DesktopShapeImpl());
        desktopCircle.draw(); // draws circle on desktop

        Shape webSquare = new Square(new WebShapeImpl());
        webSquare.draw(); // draws square on web
    }
}
```

In this example, the Shape abstraction defines the draw() method, which is implemented by the Circle, Square and Triangle classes. The ShapeImpl interface defines the methods for drawing each shape on a specific platform, which are implemented by the DesktopShapeImpl and WebShapeImpl classes. The bridge between the abstraction and implementation is established by passing an implementation object to the Shape constructor.

By using the Bridge pattern, we have decoupled the abstraction from its implementation, allowing us to add new shapes or platforms by creating new implementation classes that adhere to the platform-specific interface, without changing the existing code. This makes it easier to manage multiple dimensions of variability and extensibility in complex system architectures.

6.18 Analyze the role of the Template Method pattern in designing extensible and maintainable frameworks, libraries, or platforms with a high level of customization and complexity.

The Template Method pattern is a behavioral design pattern that allows for the creation of a high-level algorithm that defines the steps of an operation, but provides the ability to customize some of the steps through subclasses. This pattern plays a crucial role in designing extensible and maintainable frameworks, libraries, or platforms with a high level of customization and complexity.

A framework that uses the Template Method pattern provides a high-level implementation that takes care of the overall process while allowing customization of certain steps. This approach simplifies the implementation and maintenance of the framework, as well as making it more flexible to changes in the requirements.

For instance, let's assume we are developing a game engine that
has several game objects, each with different behavior. The
game engine should have a consistent way of handling each
game object, but some objects may require custom behavior.
The Template Method pattern can be used in this scenario to
provide a high-level algorithm that describes the process of handling game objects, the game engine can call this algorithm on
each game object. However, it can allow customization of certain methods through subclassing. This ensures that game objects behavior can be easily customized while still maintaining
the consistency of the game engine.

Here's a Java example:

```java
public abstract class GameObject {
    public void handle() {
        start();
        update();
        if (shouldCollide()) {
            collide();
        }
        end();
    }

    protected abstract void start();

    protected abstract void update();

    protected abstract void collide();

    protected void end() {
        // some implementation
    }

    protected boolean shouldCollide() {
        return true;
    }
}
public class Wall extends GameObject {
    @Override
    protected void start() {
        // some implementation
    }

    @Override
    protected void update() {
```

```
        // some implementation
    }

    @Override
    protected void collide() {
        // some implementation
    }
}
public class Player extends GameObject {
    @Override
    protected void start() {
        // some implementation
    }

    @Override
    protected void update() {
        // some implementation
    }

    @Override
    protected void collide() {
        // player should not collide with other
    }

    @Override
    protected boolean shouldCollide() {
        return false;
    }
}
```

In the above example 'GameObject' class provides a template method called 'handle' that defines the steps that need to be performed on each game object. It provides the flexibility to customize the behaviors of a specific game object by allowing the subclass to implement the abstract methods. The 'Wall' class is an example of a game object with standard behavior, while 'Player' class is a game object that doesn't collide with other game objects.

The Template Method pattern helps in designing a consistent framework, library, or platform for building complex systems by providing a high-level algorithm that can be customized in specific subclasses. This allows for a flexible and maintainable codebase that can easily incorporate changes in the requirements.

6.19 Discuss the impact of the Abstract Factory pattern on system design when dealing with evolving product families or a large number of related components.

The Abstract Factory pattern is a creational design pattern that provides an interface for creating families of related or dependent objects without specifying their concrete classes. The primary motivation behind using the Abstract Factory pattern is to separate the creation of objects from their usage, allowing the system to be more flexible and adaptable to changing requirements.

When dealing with evolving product families or a large number of related components, the use of the Abstract Factory pattern can have a significant impact on system design. The following are some of the benefits of using the Abstract Factory pattern in such scenarios:

1. Promotes Loose Coupling: The Abstract Factory pattern promotes loose coupling between the client code and the concrete implementations of the product families. This means that the client code can be shielded from the details of how the objects are created, which makes the system more flexible and easier to maintain. The client code only needs to work with the abstract interfaces provided by the factory, which can be easily replaced with a different implementation if required.

2. Supports Product Evolution: The Abstract Factory pattern can be used to support product evolution by allowing the creation of new product families or components without modifying the existing client code. This means that new features or products can be added to the system without breaking the existing code, which is crucial in maintaining the integrity of the system.

3. Simplifies Component Management: The Abstract Factory pattern simplifies component management by providing a centralized location for creating and managing related components. This means that component dependencies are managed in one place, which helps to reduce complexity and increase maintainability.

Here is an example of how the Abstract Factory pattern can be used to manage related components:

```java
public interface WidgetFactory {
    Button createButton();
    TextField createTextField();
}

public class MacWidgetFactory implements WidgetFactory {
    public Button createButton() {
        return new MacButton();
    }
    public TextField createTextField() {
        return new MacTextField();
    }
}

public class WinWidgetFactory implements WidgetFactory {
    public Button createButton() {
        return new WinButton();
    }
    public TextField createTextField() {
        return new WinTextField();
    }
}
```

In this example, there are two concrete implementations of the 'WidgetFactory' interface: 'MacWidgetFactory' and 'WinWidgetFactory'. Each factory is responsible for creating a family of related components, such as buttons and text fields for Mac or Windows platforms. This allows the client code to work with abstract interfaces, such as 'Button' and 'TextField', instead of specific implementations. If a new product family, such as Linux, needs to be added to the system, a new 'WidgetFactory' implementation can be created without modifying the existing client code.

In conclusion, the Abstract Factory pattern is a powerful design pattern that provides a flexible and adaptable way to manage evolving product families or a large number of related components. By promoting loose coupling, supporting product evolution, and simplifying component management, the Abstract Factory pattern can help to create a robust and maintainable system.

6.20 Explain how the Visitor pattern can be adapted to support advanced traversal strategies, dynamic dispatch, or other advanced use cases in large-scale and complex object structures.

The Visitor pattern is a popular design pattern used to separate the algorithm from the structure of a composite object. It allows developers to define new operations to a composite object without modifying its structure. However, in order to support advanced traversal strategies, dynamic dispatch, or other advanced use cases in large-scale and complex object structures, the Visitor pattern needs to be adapted.

One adaptation is to use the strategy pattern to implement different traversal strategies. The strategy pattern defines a family of algorithms and encapsulates them so that they can be interchanged as needed. To implement this adaptation, different visitor objects are created to define different traversal strategies. For example, a DepthFirstVisitor may traverse a complex object structure in a depth-first manner, while a BreadthFirstVisitor may traverse it in a breadth-first manner. The abstract Visitor interface defines a method for each type of node in the composite object structure. Each concrete visitor class overrides the method for the types of nodes that it handles, and uses the strategy pattern to implement its traversal strategy.

Another adaptation is to use dynamic dispatch to determine the type of the node being visited at runtime. To accomplish this, the accept() method on each node needs to be implemented using double dispatch. Double dispatch is a technique where the type of the visitor is passed to the node being visited, and a method on the node is called to determine its type. Based on the type of the node, the correct visit method on the visitor can be called. This technique provides a way to perform dynamic dispatch and eliminates the need to use casting to determine the type of the node being visited.

Finally, the Visitor pattern can be adapted to support other advanced use cases by using the decorator pattern to add functionality to a visitor. The decorator pattern attaches additional responsibilities to an object dynamically. This allows developers to add new functionality to a visitor without changing the structure of the composite object. For example, a decorator may be added to a visitor to perform logging or validation before or after visiting each node in the composite object.

Here's an example of how the Visitor pattern can be adapted

to support dynamic dispatch:

```
public interface Node {
    public void accept(Visitor visitor);
}

public class Leaf implements Node {
    public void accept(Visitor visitor) {
        visitor.visit(this);
    }
}

public class Composite implements Node {
    private List<Node> children;

    public void accept(Visitor visitor) {
        visitor.visit(this);
        for (Node child : children) {
            child.accept(visitor);
        }
    }
}

public interface Visitor {
    public void visit(Leaf node);
    public void visit(Composite node);
}

public class DepthFirstVisitor implements Visitor {
    public void visit(Leaf node) {
        System.out.println("Visiting leaf node");
    }

    public void visit(Composite node) {
        System.out.println("Visiting composite node");
    }
}

public class Example {
    public static void main(String[] args) {
        Node node = new Composite();
        Visitor visitor = new DepthFirstVisitor();
        node.accept(visitor);
    }
}
```

In this example, the Node interface defines the accept() method,
which takes a Visitor parameter. The Leaf and Composite
classes implement this method to call the appropriate visit()
method on the visitor. The Visitor interface defines a visit()

method for each type of node in the composite object structure. The DepthFirstVisitor implements the Visitor interface
and defines a different visit() method for each type of node in
the composite object structure. Finally, the Example class creates a Composite node and a DepthFirstVisitor, and calls the
accept() method on the node to perform the traversal. The
correct visit() method is called for each node in the composite
object structure based on its type.

www.ingramcontent.com/pod-product-compliance
Lightning Source LLC
LaVergne TN
LVHW051429050326
832903LV00030BD/2992